"Paul Scott Wilson has done more than any other recent scholar to insist on the theological character of preaching through his four-pages approach to the sermon, attention to the evocative possibilities of language, and emphasis on preaching Christian doctrine. This book, written in his honor by three of his most talented students, opens even more windows on how preachers can bring the good news of a gracious and redeeming God to an increasingly troubled world."
    —RONALD J. ALLEN, Christian Theological Seminary

"*Getting to God* reminds us that sermons fail if they do not first 'get to God,' that is, point boldly to God's action in life. Since God's action is never abstract, the authors also sharpen our attention to the very particular contexts of preaching. Thus, by guiding those of us who preach to 'get to God,' they free us to preach in ways that show how 'God gets to us.' A stimulating and much-needed volume!"
    —THOMAS G. LONG, Candler School of Theology

GETTING TO GOD

GETTING TO GOD

Preaching Good News in a Troubled World

*Joni S. Sancken, Luke A. Powery,
and John Rottman*

FOREWORD BY
Paul Scott Wilson

CASCADE *Books* • Eugene, Oregon

GETTING TO GOD
Preaching Good News in a Troubled World

Cascade Books
An Imprint of Wipf and Stock Publishers
199 W. 8th Ave., Suite 3
Eugene, OR 97401

www.wipfandstock.com

PAPERBACK ISBN: 978-1-6667-3749-3
HARDCOVER ISBN: 978-1-6667-9699-5
EBOOK ISBN: 978-1-6667-9700-8

Cataloguing-in-Publication data:

Names: Sancken, Joni S., author. | Powery, Luke A., author. | Rottman,
    John, author. | Foreword by Paul Scott Wilson.
Title: Getting to God : preaching good news in a troubled world / Joni S.
    Sancken, Luke A. Powery, and John Rottman.
Description: Eugene, OR: Cascade Books, 2023 | Includes bibliographical
    references.
Identifiers: ISBN 978-1-6667-3749-3 (paperback) | ISBN 978-1-6667-9699-5
    (hardcover) | ISBN 978-1-6667-9700-8 (ebook)
Subjects: LCSH: Preaching.
Classification: BV4211.3 G50 2023 (print) | BV4211 (ebook)

For Paul Scott Wilson, our teacher, mentor, and friend.

And he said unto me, "My grace is sufficient for thee."

(2 COR 12:9 KJV)

Contents

Contents

Foreword

THE HISTORY OF THE church with its various divisions is an on-going struggle for how best to read the Bible. The issue is urgent today because of a widespread tendency: preachers commonly and unintentionally end up presenting God as a minor character in the Bible. The focus of the sermon becomes the history behind a text, the troubles of today's world, and what listeners are to do. These matters are important, but scarce time is devoted to what each text tells us about God and the gospel. If preachers and church leaders do not point to God, it may be hard for faith to increase.

Joni Sancken, Luke Powery, John Rottman, and numerous contributors to this volume are attuned to this problem. They have journeyed with me in my teaching and writing, not least in *The Four Pages of the Sermon* that asks, "How do we get to God in sermons?" These authors explore getting to God from their various social contexts, largely against the backdrop of COVID-19 and current polarization in politics. They emerge with exciting new possibilities for naming God. The lessons they draw apply far beyond their own social and cultural situations. They apply to all of us who follow Christ. They point to the urgency of speaking God to broken people and giving hope.

Why is getting to God in sermons even an issue? Isn't it enough that churches base sermons on the Bible? Is a sermon on the Bible not about God? I used to think so, before I started teaching preaching. When one has the privilege of listening to sermon after sermon, class after class, one starts to see certain patterns and trends that might not otherwise be noted. I loved my students, I wanted them to do well, and most were following good things that others on the seminary faculty and I taught. However, often I found myself working too hard: just listening, or finding positive things to encourage them, or naming what might make their preaching seem less like work for everyone. Their sermons, like many I have preached, were mostly joyless instructions to be good Christians. We all need to be occasionally reminded that we sing, "There Is a Balm In Gilead", not "Come to me, all of you, and I will weigh you down."

The Bible is our authority and guide, so we seek in it what God desires by way of repentance and new direction, and then apply it to today. Most preachers are good at this; it is called exposition and application. In *The Four Pages* I call it Page One and Page Two of the sermon. However, these Pages are mostly trouble; they make demands we cannot meet on our own, either as individuals or as a society. In trying, likely we will fail as Israel did, because we sin, evil exists, and we live in a fallen world. Furthermore, instructions and laws on their own can never add up to the gospel. From my early preaching classes I often emerged asking, where is the help? Does the coming of God in Jesus Christ make a difference for today?

People have a burden put on them on Pages One and Two, and that can be good because something has to change. That becomes a problem, however, if the sermon ends there. If people are told what to do, they cannot simultaneously focus on what God does to help them do it. A second exposition of the text is needed to look for God, that in turn will be applied. Specifically, Page Three answers, What is God doing in or behind the text? A text may mention God directly in one of the persons of the Trinity, or God may be behind it in the larger context. The second movement from exegesis to application is Pages Three and Four.

These Pages are not new to preaching; they have been part of its practice from the early church. They have just not always been set apart, acknowledged, described, advocated, or made intentional. They constitute an essential grammar that allows the gospel to be proclaimed. The Pages can be roughly equal in length, because they are of equal importance. They move to grace, though they can be ordered in various ways.

God's saving help is present throughout the Bible and is most clearly seen in the Christ event: the coming of God in Jesus, his rising from the dead, his presence with us now in the Spirit, and his return at the end of time to fulfill all of God's promises. The hope from any text, once lifted up, can be magnified by connecting it especially to the resurrection and gift of the Spirit.

Through God being proclaimed, people find reason to hope and celebrate. God is now not just mentioned in passing, roughly half of the sermon discusses God's action in the Bible and today. The pages move from law to gospel (or trouble to grace), mirroring the overall movement of faith from the exodus to the return to the promised land, or Good Friday to Easter. Other movements in the Bible are not our model because they describe sin or backsliding, not the gospel and faith.

Is it necessary to be so intentional in using a grammar for the gospel? We could be like a student who once came to preaching class, pleased with himself for being unprepared. He argued from Luke 12:12 that the Spirit will give words to say. The professor said to him, "When Jesus was tempted to throw himself off the parapet and let the angels bear him up, he resisted the temptation, and so should you."

At a church meeting the subject of church decline was discussed. After a few minutes of conversation, a laywoman who had been silent spoke up: "You are talking as though it is up to us to do something about the decline." Maybe she was saying something many of us have heard: "Volunteer organizations in our society are all facings difficulties, as is the church. Decline is a fact of life. Accept it." Or maybe she was saying, "It is up to church leaders to give more direction to the church." Or perhaps she was making a theological statement—"The church still belongs to God and God is still in control. It is not up to us to save the church."

She could have been right on all three counts, yet all Christians are called to foster faith by pointing to who God is and what

God does. Divine action is not something we imagine out of thin air. We start with a Bible text. God is already the main character, even if common readings often ignore this. In the midst of whatever struggles the text illumines, God is doing something to help those in trouble. That is Page Three, grace in the biblical text, and it is the foundation for a move to Page Four, grace in the world.

Page Four can be the most difficult to compose—in order to be authentic, it takes time, theological discernment, good stories, and pastoral skill. Here the whole sermon comes together. It is risky because in faith the preacher dares to name the handiwork of God in world events. John the Baptist pointed a long finger to Jesus approaching through the desert crowd and said, "Here is the Lamb of God who takes away the sin of the world" (John 1:29). In spite of the danger for preachers of getting God wrong, they nonetheless stand on solid ground in pointing with John the Baptist, because Scripture is the guide. What God did then, God may be trusted to do today, for "Jesus Christ is the same yesterday and today and forever" (Heb 13:8). As the authors of this book confirm, "God shows up in and through the lives of real people in real places of brokenness and possibility."

How we name God in the particular contexts of our lives and ministry is the subject of this volume. What a journey Sancken, Powery, and Rottman take us on as they deal with tough situations: secularism in Ohio, racism and racial tensions at Duke University, and prison life in Louisiana and Michigan. Amazingly, they describe these in Celtic terms as "thin places," places where barely a veil separates the physical and the spiritual, earth and heaven—one might think of the restored medieval chapel under clear skies on the island of Iona in Scotland. Here, however, thin places name God in the grittiness of troubled life, suffering, shepherding, saving, and providing sustaining hope, each day sufficient unto itself.

Readers will find here renewed faith and passion for preaching. I love that the authors provide a treasury of wonderful and often moving stories that powerfully bolster faith and that will need to be told and retold, again and again. Even more, they model how we can all be more attentive to the actions of the awe-inspiring One at whose feet we kneel in worship.

I am deeply honored by this project, and I extend my sincere thanks to the authors for their labors here in getting to God. They have beautiful deep faith and I rejoice in calling them friends. Thus I know that for them, the silent and most important dedication of this book is to God.

Paul Scott Wilson
Professor Emeritus of Homiletics
Emmanuel College
University of Toronto

Acknowledgments

WE HAVE MANY PEOPLE to thank for their support and inspiration with this project. We are grateful to the leadership and institutions where we serve: United Theology Seminary; Duke University, particularly Duke Chapel and Duke Divinity that blessed Luke with a sabbatical during which this book was written; and Calvin Theological Seminary.

We extend thanks to the students, pastors, individuals, groups, and colleagues in the Academy of Homiletics who have nourished our research and graciously provided sermon examples for chapter 5. We especially acknowledge the Calvin Prison Initiative and the inmate clergy leadership at Ionia and Angola prisons, the Lester Randall Preaching Fellowship, the pastoral staff and members of Fairmont Presbyterian Church in Kettering, Ohio, students Rachel Latimer and Mark Vorencamp for early proofreading, Dr. Eric Rottman for help with our bibliography, Don McCrory for formatting and editorial work, Steve Schumm for last-minute help with footnotes, Scott Hoezee, Calvin Center for Excellence in Preaching, the staff and editors at Wipf and Stock who signed onto this project, and Ron Allen who had the idea for this book and nudged us forward.

We are indebted to the love, support, and patience of our families, who carved out quiet and space for our frequent Zoom meetings and writing time amidst the extra stress of homeschooling children and sheltering in place as COVID-19 closed our schools and local writing haunts.

ACKNOWLEDGMENTS

This book was written, in part, to honor Paul Scott Wilson on the occasion of his retirement from teaching at Emmanuel College after thirty-four years. His ministry, teaching, writing, leadership in our guild, and friendship have deeply influenced us and the field of homiletics. We are so thankful for Paul!

Joni S. Sancken
Luke A. Powery
John Rottman

Introduction

THIS BOOK HAS BEEN a labor of love to honor Paul Scott Wilson's many contributions to the church and academy. We were his doctoral students at Emmanuel College and have continued to appreciate his support, friendship, mentoring, and wise counsel. Although we represent different perspectives and diverse backgrounds, we share some very important theological DNA from our formation with Paul Wilson. As we worked together on a theme and direction for this book, we surveyed other former students and teaching colleagues. Very quickly, a dominant vision emerged.

Paul Scott Wilson's work has been laser focused on keeping God at the center of preaching. For Paul Wilson, a sermon must "get to God." His writing spans aspects of preaching, including history of preaching, biblical interpretation, theology of preaching, and a holistic method for sermon creation grounded in a theological grammar that uses the energy of the gospel itself. His approach to preaching uses "trouble" and "grace" to create "pages" of the sermon that engage the biblical text and our world with an explicit focus on God's gracious action that moves toward us.

This book builds on Wilson's work by focusing on the challenges and possibilities for preachers who are trying to get to God in the midst of varied contextual challenges and particularities. For the purposes of this book, a sermon "gets to God" when preachers explicitly name God's action in our world through example or story. Getting to God is possible only because God is always getting to us, and our job as preachers is to bear witness as an act of confession and spiritual discipline.

In chapter 1, we frame our understanding of the purpose of preaching as getting to God, offering metaphors and naming common challenges preachers face. We also introduce our own preaching contexts, which are integral to the following chapters. We were writing this book in the spring of 2020, while the world was caught in the emerging pain, fear, and suffering caused by COVID-19. Communities around the world were also rocked by anguished protests surrounding racial injustice and the killing of unarmed Black people. These events have affected every preaching context.

In chapters 2 through 4, each author engages with her or his preaching context with a focus on getting to God. Each chapter offers an introduction to the context, challenges, and possibilities for preachers, and a case study sermon preached in that context. Joni Sancken writes about secularism in suburban Ohio, Luke Powery writes about racism at Duke University, and John Rottman writes about prison, a place marked both by despair and suffering and the presence of Christ.

Chapter 5 unfolds as a celebration of diverse ways preachers get to God in particular contexts and features many sermon examples representing a range of perspectives and backgrounds.

We can trust that God shows up in and through the lives of real people in real places of brokenness and possibility. In Wilson's "four-page" sermon, "page four" focuses on the living God's gracious action in our world.[1] A life spent looking at the world with an eye toward "page four" can be profoundly transformative for preachers and congregations. God's promises are not general news for generic people. God's promises are good news for all people in a variety of contexts, revealing that there is still good news in a troubled world.

---

1. Wilson, *Four Pages*.

I

Getting to God

Getting to God as the Purpose of Preaching

THIS BOOK STARTS WITH the premise that Christian preaching should bear witness to the triune God. In fact, the entire act of preaching should be a God-soaked venture: the study of Scripture or topic, preparation, the interweaving of poetry and story, engagement with the listening community and broader context as partners in preaching, the design of worship, and the embodied act of proclamation itself. If we could condense the God-soaked journey of preaching down to one saturated and concentrated destination, it is this: preaching needs to get to God. While we cannot control the living and active God, we acknowledge that human preachers have a calling to bear witness to the gospel, the good news most fully expressed in the Christ event.

The gospel is a multifaceted jewel. It is overwhelming with its dazzling brilliance all at once, but preaching is an incremental task, a relationship that unfolds over time. Diverse angles and edges shine when sermons explore different possibilities. Sermons can teach, offer ethical guidance, rally the community to act in the face of injustice, and validate the human experience. Perhaps the highest aim, though, is to create conditions where listeners might

1

experience an encounter with the living God to whom we bear witness.

Like a well-trained jeweler, the preacher highlights God's activity. Sometimes the biblical text illuminates experiences in our context and at other times our lives and experiences from our world enlighten the text in a kind of mutually beneficial hermeneutical dance. Sermons that place God's action at the heart and utilize stories and examples that show us where God is active in our world today can help to inspire hope, nurture faith, and create conditions where listeners are able to see God at work in their lives. The goal is inviting or facilitating a homiletical Holy Spirit mediated encounter with God that fortifies and transforms listeners, launching them to faithfully live out the mission of God.

While this is the high calling of preaching, it is not easily accomplished. Naming God in ordinary times is hard enough, and in times of a world pandemic and racial upheaval it may seem almost impossible. At the time of this writing, COVID-19 is sowing illness, devastation, and death as it holds the world in its grip of fear. Economic, political, social, and spiritual fallout from the virus has laid bare injustices that have long simmered in the background. On top of that, the killings of George Floyd, Ahmaud Arbery, and Breonna Taylor, three Black human beings, have incited racial anger and triggered deep trauma that is boiling over in cities and towns around the world.

In the midst of these crises, church leaders must blaze new trails in ministry, embrace technology, and tackle ever changing barriers in worship and caregiving, while managing their own fear, anxiety, grief, rage, and health. The age-old challenge of how to name God in our world looms large. As Paul Scott Wilson has written, "Many of us [are] stretched to our limits and thin in resources upon which to draw, yet we are called to lead our people where none of us has been before."[1]

The situation we face is unprecedented but deeply resonant with the heart of the Christian gospel. Our God knows what it is like to watch his beloved Son gasp his final breath in a public

1. Wilson, "Thin Resources."

lynching designed to humiliate and terrorize. Our God in Jesus Christ has also traveled the way of suffering, death, and loss. Jesus absorbed, deactivated, and ultimately defeated all forces that destroy creaturely flourishing. The crucified and risen Christ is drawing near to us even now. In the midst of deep trouble, God generates new and creative ways to break through the fear and pain to get to us even as we seek to get to God.

Getting to God and the Biblical Text

Each year seminary students and many pastors travel to the Middle East, hoping to gain insight into biblical interpretation from "walking where Jesus walked." John recently traveled with a group of students to Turkey and Greece. The aim of the trip was to visit places highlighted in the New Testament. Because of his work teaching in prison, he was especially eager to see Philippi. Philippi promised possible engagement with the best prison story in the Bible, the ancient setting of God's springing Paul and Silas from the slammer through a powerful earthquake.

The ancient sites varied in scope and degrees of development. For instance, archaeologists have been at work in Ephesus for more than a hundred years. Thus, much has been uncovered. Most sites feature ancient baths, marketplaces, temples to various gods, wrecked fountains, and giant theaters, mostly in profound states of disrepair. Most temples, for example, present only a smattering of marble foundation stones with a couple of lonely pillars reaching toward a nonexistent roof. The guide was forever encouraging the group to use their imaginations to fill in what was missing.

Unfortunately, try as they might, human excavation and imagination could not bring a living spark. Despite his efforts, John realized that these ancient sites offered little help in connecting with the divine reality mentioned in the New Testament. When his group arrived in Philippi, John was initially thrilled to see the prison where Paul and Silas famously sang the night away.[2]

2. Acts 16.

A small sign identified the prison site, with carving in the side of the rock. The thrill died away moments later as the guide dismissed the location as doubtful. The visit did very little to bring John or his students closer to the biblical text or to the jailer who probably never worked there, let alone the God who shook the place to its foundations. Getting to God, even God "back then," faced insurmountable obstacles.

Historical criticism has taught preachers to excavate biblical texts with similar hopes for bringing them back to life. Preachers were prompted to sift through biblical texts from a growing distance of nearly two thousand years, to unearth historical details and use them as best they could to imagine what might have been. The idea was to clear away centuries of theological debris in an effort to get back to ancient historical biblical foundations. And with the minimal rendering of what they unearth, this prompted preachers to see themselves mostly as cautious tour guides of these excavated biblical texts.

Worshippers may come hoping to "encounter God" or "meet Jesus," but often the morning sermon leaves them with little more than a historical rendering of a text bereft of its life and vitality, without much or any mention of God.[3] One of us heard a listener comment recently on such a sermon in the church basement after the service. "Wasn't that a wonderful sermon," she cooed. "I learned so much about Pontius Pilate." Those who had longed for an encounter with the living God were not helped by such a sermon. Particularly today, when our world is racked with pain, illness, injustice, and upheaval, listeners deserve more.

If preachers too often offer their listeners only the barest possibility of accessing God through the portal of the ancient text, looking for God in particular contemporary contexts might leave both preacher and listener even more daunted. Contexts matter because, at their best, preachers must work not just to understand a biblical text, but also to use that text as a potential means by which the Holy Spirit might address the lives of the listeners in diverse contexts, even ones full of trouble.

3. Wilson, *God Sense*, 38.

Thin Places and Getting to God

In times of deep trouble, getting to God by naming and experiencing God through ancient practices, symbols, and ideas can bring comfort and strength. The Celtic theological concept of "thin places" may offer a fruitful way to describe God's presence with us amidst the deep challenges unearthed by the global coronavirus pandemic and the global social virus of racism.[4]

Celtic Christianity employs tensive theological metaphors to describe how God's presence draws near to us and reflects the mystery of divine revelation. As Scripture teaches, in complete freedom God can make any place a place of holy encounter, yet God also promises to be near to us in particular places and circumstances.[5] Celtic Christianity emphasizes "the essential goodness of nature, with a divine spark existing within all of creation."[6] Early Celtic spirituality embraces a sense of God's presence completely interwoven in all of human life.[7] This belief is depicted symbolically in the interwoven lines of the Celtic knot.[8]

Yet Celtic spirituality also describes the theological concept of thin places. Thin places refer to geographic locations where people feel closer to the divine; the distance between heaven and earth or God and humanity seems to be shorter. Celtic religious and spiritual practices were historically local in nature and reflected a deep sense of spiritual connection to nature and particular locations.[9] More recently, George McCleod, who engineered the rebuilding of the abbey on the island of Iona, also shared experiences of the immediate presence of God and the "thinness of the line that divides

4. Wilson, *God Sense*, 38.

5. God appears to Jacob in a dream (Gen 28:10–22) and Moses in a burning bush (Exod 3). These are unexpected thin places of revelation. Expected places of divine encounter include the temple and tabernacle.

6. Beres, "Celtic Spirituality," 102. Bradley, *Pilgrimage,* 33.

7. Beres, "Celtic Spirituality," 102.

8. Beres, "Celtic Spirituality," 102.

9. Beres, "Celtic Spirituality, 101–2.

this world and the next."[10] Iona has continued to be considered a thin place by many who travel there on spiritual pilgrimages.

Others suggest that the experience of thin places has to do more with us or our perceptions than with God actually being more present in some places. Speaker and author Eric Weiner writes that travel to thin places "disorients and confuses." When we are out of our usual routines we may "stumble upon" a thin place.[11] Places become "thin" to us when we are vulnerable and open to God, when we set aside our pretense of control. Weiner writes, "If God (however defined) is everywhere and 'everywhen' as the Australian aboriginals put it so wonderfully, then why are some places thin and others not? Why isn't the whole world thin? Maybe it is because we're too thick to recognize it. Maybe thin places offer glimpses not of heaven but of earth as it really is, unencumbered, unmasked."[12]

Some surmise that part of the popularity of pilgrimage to holy places has to do with a deep desire to have an "unmediated" encounter with the divine, without clergy or leaders facilitating or getting in the way.[13] Jesus himself sought out deserted places to pray. Yet communal worship and particularly the sermon can be a thin place, a place to come with openness and a place to experience a transforming encounter with God.

This book engages the tensive energy of how God comes to us in both expected and unexpected ways in the particularities of local context and the challenges that preachers face in naming God's presence. The sermon represents a potential thin place where the distance between God and our lives becomes closer and where we may experience a transformative encounter with the divine. These thin places are deeply contextual. Our perceptions, cultures, limitations, and needs mediate our experiences of God's active presence in our world while God meets us in our vulnerability.

10. Beres, "Celtic Spirituality, 101–2. Bradley, *Pilgrimage,* 108.
11. Weiner, "Heaven and Earth."
12. Weiner, "Heaven and Earth."
13. Beres, "Celtic Spirituality," 102.

The Challenge of Getting to God

This dynamic between the human and divine is intrinsic to preaching and at times seems to offer a maddening lack of clarity when it comes to naming God's presence in our world. This lack of clarity is intense for preachers today, who are facing bad news and trouble on an unprecedented scale amidst the pandemic caused by the coronavirus and other social challenges. The world is facing a health crisis of unimaginable scope, our cities echo with the wails of ambulances, millions suffer loss of income that threatens their security at the most basic of levels. Every generation is experiencing trauma and loss: loss of graduation celebrations and birthday parties, death itself and the inability to be present with loved ones in the moment of death or to mark their lives with funerals. Moreover, the pandemic is deepening fissures related to white privilege, wealth, access to health care, and gender disparity. These circumstances amplify the challenge facing preachers but also deepen the need for the gospel.

Preachers face significant challenges. Brokenness, suffering, pain, loss, tragedy, and injustice lay bare human finitude and sin. At times these experiences contribute to a thin place where people meet God, but these experiences can also make it hard to see where God is working in our world as we get bogged down in our own limitations and grief. In their recent book, *The Power of Bad*, social scientists John Tierney and Roy Baumeister explore the weight that negative events or experiences have in people's lives.[14] Tierney and Baumeister posit that we need many more good things or good experiences to balance the power of even one negative experience.[15] Many of us can attest to this in minor or significant ways. One criticism can often overrule many compliments, and sadly, one traumatic childhood experience can often haunt entire lives. In our preaching the negativity effect takes hold when we name trouble, sin, and brokenness, and aren't able to offer enough examples of good news to leave listeners with a sense of

14. Tierney and Baumeister, *Power of Bad*, 23.
15. Jacobsen and Kelly, *Kairos Preaching*, 9.

hope. When preachers are discerning God's action in our world, they also experience the negativity effect, which makes it difficult to see God's actions in our world as tipping the scale toward hope.

There tends to be a sense that truly good news is a scarce commodity, and incidents of God's action are rare. Indeed, we struggled with this very challenge in our work on this book as two of our contributors used the same story in their sermons. Powerful stories of God's action circulate on the internet and find new life in many sermons. God is magnified by this witness but there are many more stories of God's action to be proclaimed. The negativity effect can blind us to the abundance of God's presence.

Another challenge is the matter of perception in naming events in our world as God's action. We live in an age of contested sources of authority. What a preacher names as God's action, someone else may name as something else. There are usually many plausible explanations. While we may be preaching to believers in our congregations or to people curious enough to come to church, we have friends and loved ones who do not believe in God or who may believe in a God who is not active in our world but rather a God who put an order in place that unfolds largely without intervention, a "Bette Midler God" who is "watching us from a distance."

The Significance of Context for Preaching

Because this book will be dealing with the challenges of preaching in particular contexts, defining what we mean when we talk about context may provide some clarity of purpose. In *Kairos Preaching,* David Schnasa Jacobsen and Robert Kelly helpfully delineate between the terms "context" and "situation."[16] *Context* refers to "enduring social, cultural, and political features that color the ways in which we who live in the North American context hear the gospel," while *situation* is "a moment or crisis that evokes a sense of limit/

---

16. Jacobsen and Kelly, *Kairos Preaching,* 9.

finitude or calls forth a decision."[17] Preaching is an event that not only reflects and responds to context, but also contributes to shaping that context. Every part of the sermon is deeply contextual. No word can be proclaimed in a vacuum. There are many diverse contexts within North America. The Latin root for the word "context" involves a sense of "weaving together."[18] Whole books have been written on contextual theologies. What we offer here is not by any means exhaustive but intended as an example of preachers who are already deeply immersed in particular contexts while seeking to preach the good news that explicitly names God as an active agent in our world amidst complexities and challenges associated with that particular preaching context.

COVID-19 in Our Contexts

Holy Week 2020 was a historic experience for global Christians who travelled our most sacred journey to Jesus' cross and resurrection, yet were unable to worship together in person in the midst of the deadly coronavirus pandemic. Preachers had to grapple with many challenges as they sought to get to God and bear witness to the resurrection. We offer snapshots from Holy Week 2020 in our own voices from our contexts. These snapshots provide a foretaste of the contexts we will discuss in later chapters.

Joni Sancken writes about the ways in which secularism has created challenges for preachers in an Ohio suburb through a loss of connection with transcendence and a strong sense of personal autonomy. Yet God, who overcame the chasm between humanity and divine transcendence by becoming human in Jesus Christ, testified to in the prologue of the Gospel of John, continues to stay with us in thin places of vulnerability and compassion.

Luke Powery writes about the insidious and deep stain of racism and white supremacy active in the past and present of Duke University. As in the exodus, where God frees Israel from

---

17. Jacobsen and Kelly, *Kairos Preaching*, 9.

18. Jacobsen and Kelly, *Kairos Preaching*, 29.

enslavement, guides them to freedom with a pillar of cloud and a pillar of fire, travels with them, and surrounds a formerly enslaved, dehumanized, and devalued people with a thin place where they are continually sustained by the divine presence, Jesus draws especially near to those who experience systemic oppression.[19]

John Rottman writes about preaching in prison, a place of despair, suffering, and brokenness with many barriers to getting to God. Yet in Matthew 25:31–46, Jesus names prison as a "thin place," an expected place of encounter and connection with the divine.

Joni Sancken on Secular Suburbia and COVID-19

The threat of the novel coronavirus has shut down my suburban Ohio community. This increasingly secular community is typically marked by privilege, high-achieving schools, and successful adults, people who are used to steering their own destiny. The trauma of COVID-19 has rattled this. Shelly Rambo writes, "[T]rauma rolls back the curtain of our assumptions of autonomy, exposing this 'fleshy' insight: that we are not immune from the processes of the world but, in fact, profoundly subject to them."[20] Friends in ministry have observed that church members are seeking comfort through relationships with other people, and their longing is mostly housed in hope oriented toward favorable outcomes rather than something ontological or connected to our Christian identity. In keeping with a more secular perspective that finds less meaning in the idea of transcendence, my pastor focused the application portion of his Easter season preaching on how the risen Jesus comes to us in the midst of our ordinary days. People don't need to take a pilgrimage to find God.

I'm largely cut off physically from my suburban neighbors as we each maintain social distance from each other. Nevertheless,

19. Among other biblical passages, many psalms speak evocatively of God's special care and protection for marginalized and oppressed groups. See Pss 9:9; 10:17–18; 12:5; 68:5; 103:6; and 146:7–9, among others.

20. Rambo, *Resurrecting Wounds*, 40.

in my neighborhood, I do experience God "getting to us" through many acts of "compassionate witness" amidst the varying levels of pain, trauma, and violence caused by the coronavirus.

The concept of compassionate witness has been a powerful one for me and is a tool I have used as I work with pastors who are seeking to be more sensitive and aware of the effects of trauma in our world. In *Common Shock*, Kaethe Weingarten, former associate clinical professor of psychology in the department of psychiatry at Harvard Medical School and founder and director of the Witnessing Project, reminds us that it is a sign of our common humanity to experience a reaction to pain, trauma, and violence in our world and that far too often we stifle our response and distance ourselves from the pain of others. Acts of compassionate witness acknowledge the pain of others in a real or symbolic way and also attend to the collateral wound the suffering of another creates in us. Acts of compassionate witness involve selecting an arena of focus amidst the pain, listening and responding in a caring way, and doing something either concrete or symbolic.[21] Because the coronavirus does not discriminate and has touched humanity at large, this event makes us aware of our common humanity in profound ways.

During this pandemic, acts of compassionate witness have cropped up everywhere and in unexpected ways. At six o'clock every evening everyone comes out on their porches and visits while being socially distanced. We gather with a few neighbors in a large circle that goes into the street. My children look forward to this time of connection. This is an act of compassionate witness—it attends to the needs of others and us; it acknowledges our common humanity. During a family walk, we discovered that the teachers in my daughter's first grade class had created large signs, which they posted in the windows of the school with messages for the children. We felt seen, cared for, and loved, a sign of resurrection.

---

21. Weingarten, *Common Shock*, 192–93. See also Hunsinger, *Bearing the Unbearable*, 25. Protests around the world (including in my own community) following the deaths of unarmed African Americans can also be viewed as a form of compassionate witness.

Chalk messages of hope and peace, stuffed animals placed in windows for children to do neighborhood "safaris," and people sharing food and household goods with each other by leaving packages on porches are all signs of Christ's presence among us in this season.

These acts of compassionate witness obviously do not remove the threat of coronavirus, nor do they remove the pain that many are experiencing through physical illness, economic suffering, racism, and other hardship.[22] They do not restore a lost job, guarantee access to health care, or physically remove a person who may be stuck in their home with an abusive parent or partner. However, these actions do offer potential transformation and hope by re-establishing human connection amidst isolation.[23] They are signs, however small, that incrementally point toward creation's ultimate destination. I see acts of compassionate witness as signs of Christ among us and God's in-breaking realm, and have often pointed to actions like this in my sermons.

Recognizing humans as Christ's hands and feet is a secular-friendly way to "get to God," and represents a comfort zone for preaching the gospel in my setting. However, I also find myself longing for the transcendent in a deep way, longing for something beyond me and beyond human actions that I can explain. I am so aware of the fragility of life at present, and I long for a God who is greater and more powerful, who truly holds the whole world. Others may feel this hunger, but in the confines of our secular norms and social distancing, I don't feel comfortable shouting faith questions, sidewalk to porch. This sense of my own need represents a potential thin place.

From conversations with pastors, and my own observations, I do not see much change in the faith of Christians in my secular suburb. People do not seem to be seeking the divine in new ways. However, preaching can cultivate our desire for thin places in the ways we approach human need. In a recent email exchange, pastor Brian Maguire vividly describes his approach to gently nudging his congregation into deeper spiritual waters, "to tempt people with

22. Hunsinger, *Bearing the Unbearable*, 25.
23. Hunsinger, *Bearing the Unbearable*, 25.

tastes of transcendence that may stimulate their desire for more . . . the way famine relief workers place drops of sugar water on starving children's lips to trigger their hunger and digestive system to reactivate. For many we are so far from the transcendent that our first task seems to be to remind them what they are missing."[24]

Luke Powery on Duke and COVID-19

As with many universities and colleges, COVID-19 basically cleared Duke's campus within a relatively short period of time. From monitoring the coronavirus outbreak to travel restrictions placed on students to encouraging students to reconsider international travel on spring break to all the changes after spring break—shifting to remote online instruction; instructing students not to return to campus except in extraordinary circumstances; suspending all nonessential university-funded travel; canceling or virtualizing Duke-sponsored in-person events; limiting the number of visits to campus sites; providing remote work options for staff and faculty; cancelling the ACC basketball tournament; and closing recreation facilities, Duke Gardens, the Nasher Museum of Art, and Duke Chapel.

Eventually, we learned that some Duke community members tested positive for the coronavirus. Then, the economic impact of this virus became a reality for Duke—a notice went out that there would be no new nonsalary expenditures, including travel and entertainment, meetings and conferences; all staff hiring would be paused; no salary increases for those making more than $50,000; new construction projects put on hold; and salary cuts for highly compensated employees. The list continued to grow as COVID-19 changed the way the university operated.

It certainly changed corporate worship, as a few ministers and musicians led virtual-only services at Duke Chapel during the pandemic. One example was the Maundy Thursday service. I watched this service online while on sabbatical. At this service, the

24. Maguire, "Longing for the Transcendent?"

chapel staff wore masks for the first time. I did not see the masks as health precautions, though of course they were. I saw ministers with masks in a sanctuary for worship as a reminder that we are all like sick patients in a holy hospital, waiting to be touched by the Great Physician, although there is a governmental order for social distancing. What I saw visually proclaimed and embodied in the house of God was the message that we are all sick in some way, regardless of race or ethnicity, at least metaphorically, and for thousands now, due to the coronavirus, literally. The coronavirus has lifted this truth to the surface of our lives as all are susceptible to this virus and its impact. Many existential accoutrements have been stripped from us, and we are laid bare, naked in our human need, exposed as dust.

The Maundy Thursday liturgy mirrored life—pervasive sickness—because during this pandemic, even (in)humanity has been exposed again. The sin of racism has been revealed again. On March 24, 2020, Duke president Vincent Price sent out a message about "the importance of inclusion." It was not the typical, expected message about logistical or administrative changes due to COVID-19. Rather, he denounced the incidents against all Asians and Asian-Americans occurring in the United States due to the coronavirus outbreak. It was a message about core human and institutional values. He affirmed our common humanity and called for continual regard and respect for others. He wrote,

> The recent spate of bias incidents across America not only reflects the most misguided, distorted, and base biases about the coronavirus, it is also thwarting the public health response to the virus's spread. I want to be quite clear: Duke resoundingly condemns any discrimination or bias against our Asian or Asian-American neighbors, and we pledge to continue advocating for shared values of inclusion, mutual trust, and respect.[25]

His note was a reminder that COVID-19 is not the only virus threatening human beings, but the virus of racism continues to wreak havoc in society.

25. Price, "Importance of Inclusion."

Even during a global pandemic, racism seeks to survive and tear apart human lives. President Price's message was not a sermon, but it spoke truth about a reality that persists all over the world; even Duke is not immune. The coronavirus, though it kills people, cannot kill the virus of racism. This intense situation offers a challenge to getting to God in preaching—that is, our own human frailty and failures as creatures of God, as needy human clay who struggle with racialized realities. There is no easy way to get to God.

We are all sick in our own way, and COVID-19 is not bound by racial categories nor is it a respecter of persons. While all are susceptible to this virus, all are also susceptible to being touched by the viral love of God, regardless of one's racialized identity. This racialized sickness is real, but grace has no race attached to it; thus, the gospel is for all, oppressor and oppressed. Irrespective of race, God will pour grace on all flesh, on all people. This can be hard to see and proclaim when racism seeks to ruin God's beautiful creation. Nonetheless, we preachers hope and pray that God will get to us through governmental guidelines and ruinous racism in order to redeem the sin-sick world.

John Rottman on Prison and COVID-19

Shortly after the COVID-19 pandemic became the first thing on everyone's mind, a friend called to ask if the crisis might impact people's stance toward God. Would people turn toward or turn away from God? Might it spark some sort of great awakening? Would churches see a spike in membership, if not during the pandemic, then shortly thereafter?

I professed my shortsightedness as a prophet. God only knew whether this pandemic might prompt people to recognize thin places in their world or harden hearts in response to this natural evil's impact upon their lives. While I offered my friend no settled opinion, I did wonder how this crisis might impact the prison congregations that I knew and loved. Would they survive the assault or wither and die?

Everyone who stopped to think about it realized that inmate populations are among the world's most vulnerable. Even without a viral pandemic, prisons are incubators for emotional distress, racial tension, smothering loneliness, and violent intimidation. Trouble in the world of the incarcerated is everywhere.

Deploying tactics for fighting a deadly virus only serves to multiply those troubles. Social distancing in a place like Angola Prison (Louisiana) is all but impossible. Inmates sleep in dormitories of forty men on rows of bunk beds in rooms originally designed to hold half that many. Others in both Ionia (Michigan) and Angola prisons find themselves double bunked in long rows of cells designed for single occupancy. Consequently, these housing units are far more efficient than any cruise ship in incubating an intruding virus.

Furthermore, inmates found themselves ill-prepared to fight the intruder. Too many inmates found themselves saddled with high-carb, low-quality diets coupled with few opportunities to exercise. An absence of green vegetables and the preponderance of high-fat proteins served to nurture a host of underlying conditions making inmates especially susceptible to COVID's ravages. And while prison physicians often did their best under less-than-optimal conditions, the medical system served inmates sporadically with considerably less-than-attentive care.

All of these factors might prompt one to suppose that the COVID crisis would only serve to make such places hardly conducive to finding God in ordinary times, and now even less so. But some initial reports suggested that God might just have broken through, broken through profoundly.

Shortly after the COVID crisis hit, the Richard A. Handlon Correctional Facility in Ionia, Michigan, where Calvin University and Calvin Theological Seminary sponsor a fully accredited BA in Ministry Leadership, locked down. Professors, inmate visitors, religious volunteers, and anybody other than prison personnel were barred from entering. Many wondered how the church there behind the razor wire was doing.

Then about two weeks after the lockdown began, word began to filter out. Assistant director Kary Bosma forwarded this note to friends of the program:

> We received a note from Ken De Kleine, who serves as our CPI assistant (he's a prisoner, but not a CPI student). He sent this note regarding the ongoing worship services in the absence of outside volunteers, *"I wish you could all experience and partake in some of the joy that I feel during the services when I see and hear the preaching that some of the CPI students are doing. You all would be proud of what is happening here during this time when outside volunteers are not able to make it in to preach. If you need some encouragement, I'm telling you*—the fruit of your labor is ripening." This is such an encouragement to us, the students who've been preparing for Christian leadership roles inside the prison through CPI are being given the opportunity to preach and lead worship in those services! They are leading at a time when outside visitors are prohibited from coming in, leading their church communities and providing a pastoral presence. This is so exciting to hear!
>
> Finally, I received many notes from CPI students who want us to know they are praying for the Calvin University and Calvin Theological Seminary communities. They are praying for those of you in leadership positions making difficult decisions, in faculty positions attempting to continue teaching, in support positions providing students with learning resources, and in fundraising positions continuing to provide what's needed to keep the program going. They are praying for the health and safety of each of us, even as we pray the same for them.[26]

What seemed like an incubator for hardened hearts and callused souls looked to have become a God-enchanted thin place. Phone calls from Angola prison offered similar God-haunted rumors. The churches were flourishing. Two hundred inmate pastors

---

26. Bosma, email to supporters of the Calvin Prison Initiative.

courageously shouldered leadership, ministering to the sick, encouraging the lonely, and praying with those in the grip of fear.

This viral assault in the prison context suggests that perhaps any context can become a thin place if God decides to show up. And these stories of God's presence and power invite us as preachers to witness to God's presence and power. Quite simply, we have been called in our sermons to get to the God who has gotten to us. We are called to preach grace and to preach good news as we stand in these thin places to proclaim what God has done, is doing, and will do as we point to these things we have heard and seen.

Getting to God as a Spiritual Practice

Focusing one's preaching on getting to God or naming God's presence clearly in our world is an act of confession, a spiritual discipline that requires practice and patience. In our work with students and pastors we have invited them to enter into this discipline of looking at the world through deliberately "God-colored" lenses. Indeed, in times such as these it would be unbearable to have to look at the world without God-colored lenses. In our experience, looking for God leads to actually seeing God. If you never look for God as a preacher, you may never see God or say anything about God in a sermon. Indeed, part of the ministry of pastors is to look for God deliberately and then to bear witness by naming these divine sightings in the sermon. Submitting to this sermonic discipline can be life changing for preachers as well as for those who hear their sermons.

Recent interactions with pastors who are suffering from advanced cancer have hit this home. Even in the midst of painful treatment, suffering, and dire prognoses, these preachers continually see God and name God's presence. Through the pulpits of their written reflections and blog posts, they continue to bear witness to the God who meets them in their deepest need. The deeper the trouble, the stronger the experience of the active presence and power of the risen Christ. When one looks for God, one finds God everywhere. When one finds God, one can point the way to others.

Seeking, finding, and naming the presence of God in the midst of deep brokenness, pain, and death not only changes our spiritual outlook but also changes everything from the neural pathways of our brains to the buoyancy of our souls, increases our experience of hope, and builds resilience.[27]

In the chapters that follow, we will offer windows into our lives and practice of seeking to get to God in our preaching. These are stories of pilgrims along the way, not sages who have found solutions or answers to this immense challenge. The practice of storytelling elicits creativity and reflection in others. By hearing one story, we learn about ourselves as well as the other (our neighbor) and the sacred Other by whose grace and power we preach. We offer these experiences in a spirit of vulnerability and trust, knowing that the Holy Spirit breaks open our lives and uses even our limitations and finitude to bear witness to the active, healing, generative, transforming, and renewing power of God in our world.

Each chapter will offer an introduction to one author's preaching context as well as insights into challenges and gifts he or she experiences preaching in that context. Each chapter ends with a sample sermon as a case study.

27. Sancken, *Words That Heal*, 16.

2

Preaching in a Disenchanted World

Joni S. Sancken

In May of 2019, a record-setting eighteen tornadoes hit the area around Dayton, Ohio, where I live with my family. An EF4 tornado with estimated wind speeds of 170 miles per hour caused significant damage in the area around the seminary where I teach.[1] In the aftermath, a local pastor friend posted on social media, something along the lines of, "God isn't playing around Dayton! Listen up. God is speaking." The following Sunday, this pastor preached a fiery sermon linking the tornadoes and other events in the news to the end times, urging listeners to get right with God before it is too late. Positively, this same pastor also posted on social media in the days following the tornadoes about various relief and cleanup efforts, also ascribing these actions to the hand of God.

My friend could be right. God could have caused these tornadoes. However, climatologists also explain that tornadoes are caused by moisture, atmospheric heat, and wind shear.[2] Further, there has been increasing discussion as to whether human-caused climate change may be playing a role in extreme weather events

1. Londberg, "Memorial Day tornadoes."
2. Chow, "What's fueling the tornados?"

20

like this.[3] Certainly, humans are behind local environmental changes caused by increased urbanization and population density. Tornadoes are more destructive when they hit an urban area than when they hit less-populated areas.

While I confess to finding the climatologists' explanation more credible in this instance, I can understand why my friend turned to God to explain the destruction. As a person of faith, I fear the hollowness of a world where terrible things "just happen," where suffering and blessing are reduced to luck and life choices that teeter on the edge of meaninglessness. I find comfort in scriptural promises that God is in charge of the forces at play in our world and that God oversees all life with intentionality.[4] I believe the words of the spiritual, "He's got the whole world in his hands. He's got the wind and the rain in his hands . . ." How do preachers proclaim amidst competing truth claims? How do we remain clear-eyed and full of faith, or, to borrow language from the Gospel of Matthew in Jesus' commissioning of the disciples, how do we preach with the wisdom of snakes and the innocence of doves?[5]

At one time, our world was dripping with connections to the transcendent. Even amidst competing divisions in the church and struggles with faith, flat-out unbelief was rare.[6] Attributing events such as natural disasters and neighborly behavior to the hand of God was common. One need not look so far back in history to hear stories of how people prayed that God might send rain to end a drought or how God punished people through a hurricane or military loss.

Today, such comments are rare, reflecting shifting cultural norms around what Canadian philosopher Charles Taylor calls "conditions for belief" and "sources of ultimate authority," hallmarks of a secular age.[7] Secularism isn't some-

3. Achenbach and Samenow, "Extreme Weather."

4. Among other psalms, see Psalm 139:16. This theology is deeply ingrained in the book of Job; see Job 26:8–9.

5. Matthew 10:16.

6. See also Smith, *How (Not) to Be Secular*, 27.

7. I prioritize the language of secularism or secularity, but literature

thing that is "out there"; it's not something that faith-filled, "He's-got-the-whole-world-in-his-hands" Christians can decide to shrug off like a sweater. Secularism is all around us—it *is* us, and it has necessarily affected preaching at a deep level.

Our present secular context for preaching is rich with possibility and gifts but preaching amidst contested sources of ultimate authority can make it hard for preachers to "get to God" with authenticity and depth. In many churches, powerful truth claims that lie at the heart of the historic Christian faith are debated. As our broader culture grows increasingly less attuned to the rhythms, narratives, and beliefs that undergird Christian faith, how can preachers preach words that build up and nurture faith while also taking secular culture seriously *on its own terms*? David Schnasa Jacobsen sees this world as

> good enough: a disenchanted place where vocations can be lived out and where ordinariness itself can be affirmed. . . . a place where Christians, led by the gospel promise in Word and Sacrament are freed to engage in practices of public hospitality and, yes, perhaps even "evangelical conversation and life on behalf of the world" again.[8] Such hospitality cannot be a means, just as the conversation cannot be a ruse for domination. Somehow we all must see that the gospel pulls us forward into deeper connection with God's good creation.[9]

A desire to take the world seriously on its own terms is part of the challenge of preaching in the context of secularism. Another side of this relational dynamic cuts to the existential heart of proclamation today. Can church be relevant in such a way that preaching matters for this disenchanted world that God loves?[10]

---

addressing the same concerns often uses other terms which offer nuances, which I use when engaging those resources, for example, "postmodern" and "postsecular."

8. Jacobsen quotes from Keifert, *Welcoming the Stranger*, 91.

9. Jacobsen, "Going Public," 381.

10. God loves the world so much that God in Christ gave God's life for it. Relationally, one may think of evangelical preaching that seeks to call others to God as external pulpits built on the outside of old cathedrals, or of worship as

Because secularism is already the context for our preaching, in some ways this chapter doesn't reveal anything new. However, Charles Taylor's account and language does call attention to aspects of our preaching method that would otherwise go unnoticed and helps to explain some of the challenges that this generation of preachers is facing.

This book asserts that "getting to God" in the sermon is vital in the Christian formation of listeners and the calling of the church. This is especially true in our disenchanted world where even believers may not readily see God at work. Preachers have the opportunity to highlight and bear witness to God's active presence in our world, to provide comfort in times of suffering and uncertainty, and to link our lives and actions to ultimate significance. Naming God's action in our sermons has powerful transformative potential; it is arguably the most important and one of the most difficult aspects of preaching.

Context: Secularism

In my suburban Ohio neighborhood, people of faith keep their religious affiliations from leaching into our shared common world. For example, in my neighborhood, practitioners of different faiths (and no faith) live and work alongside each other peacefully. Naming deeply held convictions often feels risky, and the faith leaders in our community engage with their own congregations almost entirely in isolation from each other and from our nonreligious neighbors.

My non-Christian neighbors remind me that they still must contend with feeling like "others and outsiders" in what seems like a predominantly Christian context. I honor their experiences; the dregs of Christendom still cling to the surface. But increasingly I have neighbors and friends who find meaning in life completely apart from any religion. In my local Starbucks, I spotted a young adult with a T-shirt reading "Blessed and Obsessed." I assumed it

---

a public witness that extends to the world.

was a religious shirt but when she approached my table, I noticed that rather than "God" the shirt actually said, "My Dog." Silly example aside, it can be excruciating to engage in meaningful conversation with close friends who do not believe in God in seasons of immense joy and deep sorrow. Similarly, it can also be challenging to preach to people who exist completely in the immanent world, with little sense of transcendence, who view themselves as entirely self-possessed and autonomous. What we offer doesn't feel complete; we feel something lacking.

Theological reductions related to secularism cut across all traditions within Christianity. The ways we understand belief and our role as Christian witnesses have been deeply affected by secularism. The contemporary hymn, "People Need the Lord," provides an apt example.[11] While this lyrical statement is true, in a sense it reduces Jesus to an object that believers are called to share or give to those who are hurting: "We are called to take His light to a world where wrong seems right. What could be too great a cost, for sharing life with one who's lost?"[12] Manipulating objects is the stuff of the immanent natural world. Transcendence is slippery.

Taylor describes secularism in three broad ways. The first is a "classical" understanding of the difference between particular "earthly" activities after the fall.[13] James K. A. Smith puts this in medieval terms: while the priest follows a sacred vocation, "the butcher, baker and candlestick maker are engaged in secular pursuits."[14] He also notes that for Augustine, secular has to do with an understanding of time—the time between the fall and the fulfillment of God's realm among us can be considered "secular time."[15]

Another aspect of secularism concerns the relationship between religion and public spaces and the wane of Christendom. Taylor notes that references to God or any "ultimate reality"

11. Nelson and McHugh, "People Need the Lord."
12. Nelson and McHugh, "People Need the Lord."
13. Taylor, *Secular Age*, 1–2; Smith, *How (Not) to be Secular*, 20.
14. Smith, *How (Not) to Be Secular*, 20–21.
15. Smith, *How (Not) to Be Secular*, 20.

beyond the here and now are largely absent in public spaces in the North Atlantic world.[16] We go to work or school, vote, walk the dog, attend concerts and movies, knit sweaters, play a game of pick-up basketball, and invest for retirement without necessarily referring to God or any religious beliefs.[17] This is quite different from earlier eras, when the church and Christian teaching would have dominated most aspects of life. While some may decry this more marginal voice for religious beliefs in daily life, secularism in these various spheres of life still allows believers to exercise an active faith and has allowed people of different religions and those who ascribe to no religion to live together peaceably. This being said, Taylor does note that some may mourn a time when there was more integration of faith and public life—for example, Christian prayer in public schools.[18]

The tidy separation of arenas where we talk about our faith and expect to encounter God and spaces and places where we may bracket out our beliefs creates a challenge for preachers. Creating a strict separation can hinder meaningful applications between Scripture and the traditions of the church and the everyday secular lives of listeners, or, in Paul Wilson's theological grammar, the connection between the Bible and our world.

Taylor's third understanding of secularism has even more profound implications for preaching. He also defines secularism as having contested sources of ultimate authority. As the logic goes, at one time, belief in God was uncontested, but now Christian beliefs are considered to be "one option among others, and frequently not the easiest to embrace."[19] Taylor describes a perspective likely held by most clergy as well as the members of congregations. He writes, "I may find it inconceivable that I would abandon my faith, but there are others, including possibly some very close to me, whose way of living I cannot in all honesty just dismiss as depraved, or blind, or unworthy, who have no faith (at least not in God, or the

---

16. Taylor, *Secular Age*, 1–2.
17. Taylor, *Secular Age*, 2.
18. Taylor, *Secular Age*, 2.
19. Taylor, *Secular Age*, 3.

transcendent.)"[20] The rise of the possibility of exclusive humanism coupled with a turn away from transcendence has led to our ability to "construct meaning and significance without any reference to the divine or transcendence."[21] For pastors, this saturating sense of the secular is an implicit and often unexamined but inescapable part of our preaching contexts.[22] To reiterate, it's not so much how secularism has affected *what* we believe but how it has affected *the conditions* for belief.[23] Secularism reveals that what we simply take for granted has permeated us at a level often beyond self-awareness.[24]

In addition to the privatization of faith and contested means of authority, according to Charles Taylor, our secular age is marked by distinct attributes that differ from the premodern world. We live in a disenchanted world where meaning is made internally.[25] Belief tends to be individual rather than communal. There is a collapsed sense of the ultimate good, marked by a lack of tension between the highest Christian calling and normal life.[26] Time itself and our broader understanding of the cosmos have been distilled into natural processes that unfold without mystery.[27] These attributes affect preaching, from the way we explore Scripture to the theological shape of the sermon and the stories we use.

20. Taylor, *Secular Age*, 3.
21. Smith, *How (Not) to be Secular*, 26.
22. Smith, *How (Not) to be Secular*, 26.
23. Smith, *How (Not) to be Secular*, 20.
24. Smith, *How (Not) to be Secular*, 28.
25. Smith, *How (Not) to be Secular*, 28–30.
26. Smith, *How (Not) to be Secular*, 31–33.
27. Smith, *How (Not) to be Secular*, 34–35.

Challenges and Possibilities for Preachers

Challenges

Listeners as "buffered selves"

Premodern people lived in a world where certain objects could commonly be charged with possibility, and the human self was considered more "porous" and less autonomous. A religious relic could cure illness. A person could be overtaken or troubled by demons or positively entered by the Holy Spirit or actively moved by the presence of God.[28] We encounter this when we read Scripture passages that describe a person as being "possessed." Today people consider themselves more insulated internally and more autonomous, and preachers usually address a natural world understood through natural, trackable processes rather than a supernatural world where external forces beyond our conscious awareness affect us.[29] Taylor refers to this as having a "buffered self."

The buffered self is a challenge for preachers because it can limit expectations for encountering God. Listeners may miss an opportunity to experience the biblical text or event in our world in a new way because it is difficult for them to release their sense of control or autonomy. The buffered self can make us oblivious to potential thin places where the sacred beyond is present in our world. To engage this challenge and find possibility in the experience of the buffered self, preachers can focus on human need in preaching. Human need pulls back the veil of control and autonomy that help us recognize our inability and finitude.

Here is an example of the dynamics of the buffered self and human need when interpreting Scripture for preaching. Many of my preaching students explore the account of the healing of the Gerasene demoniac[30] in a way that renders this event as more relevant for secular preachers and listeners. Often they begin by framing the man's suffering as mental illness rather than demon

28. Taylor, *Secular Age*, 34–36.
29. Taylor, *Secular Age*, 34.
30. Mark 5:1–17; Luke 8:26–37.

possession, which likely feels like a more relevant concern in many congregations.

Mental illness is very common. According to the National Alliance on Mental Illness, one in five adults lives with mental illness, while one in twenty-five live with serious mental illness.[31] One in six children aged six to seventeen will experience a challenge with their mental health this year.[32] One can assume that many in my suburban context are quietly living with mental illness.

In addition to mental illness, another part of the man's suffering is caused by the community's response. He has been isolated, left alone among the tombs, in a place of death and despair. In Mark's Gospel he has been chained or restrained.[33] The community response continues to be important in this passage as it must also grapple with his restoration and their fear in the presence of Jesus, who has disrupted social order. Similarly, today many people with mental illness experience isolation and restraint in various ways. The church struggles to engage and involve members with mental illness. Shame causes people to keep their experiences hidden.

Following this interpretive line, getting to God in the sermon may involve naming Jesus' healing action and the subsequent disruption as good news for the community as well as for the man who is now "in his right mind." A sermon could also get to God with a focus on Jesus' healing and compassion toward the suffering man. The many in our congregations whose lives are touched by mental illness will resonate with this good news. While this text talks explicitly about an outside force affecting the man in the form of demon possession and Jesus' casting out the legion who have caused this man's suffering, preachers today commonly read this text through our cultural lenses of immanence and a buffered self, that is, to focus on Jesus' compassion and to call us to show compassion today.

Our "buffered" senses of personhood may inadvertently limit some avenues for healing that require vulnerability and openness

31. National Alliance on Mental Illness, "Mental Health by the Numbers."
32. National Alliance on Mental Illness, "Mental Health by the Numbers."
33. Mark 5:4.

in the presence of deep need. Mental illness has affected my own family. My sister was diagnosed with severe bipolar disorder as a young adolescent.[34] It took many years and experimenting with a wide range of medications and treatments for her to find equilibrium. In a recent conversation, my mom recounted an incident from early in my sister's illness. My sister was agitated and unable to sleep because she felt certain that demons would harm her or others in our family if she slept. After trying to reason with her, my mom knelt beside her bed and prayed aloud that Jesus would come and hold off the demons and protect my sister and our family. My sister relaxed, her breathing calmed, and she fell asleep. My mom wondered if there could be something spiritual at work as well as mental illness. Even doctors admit that there is much we don't know about how the brain works. Perhaps there is space to acknowledge permeability that can open our lives to the healing presence of God. Sermons can normalize our need before God and our inability to understand everything. There is nothing wrong with acknowledging mystery in preaching.

Lost Transcendence

A feature in *The Christian Century* invites readers to write and submit short essays inspired by a one-word prompt. I recently read entries around the word "promise."[35] While biblical concepts of promise may bring to mind covenant with God or God's abiding eschatological promises, most of these essays involved experiences of people keeping or breaking promises in relationships. Some mentioned God's hand in keeping promises, but most involved very immanent understandings of this theologically potent concept. For example, several wrote eloquently about plants bearing fruit—a relatable metaphor but one that lacks reference to transcendence. Taylor describes our disenchanted world as existing primarily in the immanent frame with some people open to the

---

34. I have permission from my sister and mother to share this story.
35. Yoder et al., "Promise."

transcendent and others closed to it, while also being "haunted" by transcendence.

For those who are open to transcendence, we understand that which is "good" as at least partly in relationship to that which is divine or ultimate.[36] This is deeply ingrained in Christianity, but there are examples from other settings too, such as recognizing reliance on a higher power to achieve sobriety in Alcoholics Anonymous or seeing the history of the United States through a lens that names God's hand in the calling of the nation state.[37]

Within many Christian traditions we may encounter a kind of push-pull relationship between immanence and transcendence. Where do we place the horizon that orients life and decision-making? We may see God as Creator, the One who wills life on earth, but we may not regularly notice or name God's continuing action and presence in our world. Theologically, some see this as problematic, but it unfolds practically Sunday by Sunday in many churches. Drained of connection to a transcendent God, much of our faith involves morality and human ethics.

In a continuing education event at my seminary, the group of pastors generally agreed that it was easier to preach about traumatic events than miraculous ones because trauma and brokenness seem so much more common—there is a frame of reference, whereas miracles exist outside our understanding of natural order. Many Christians struggle with how to integrate positive experiences of the miraculous. Taylor poetically describes miracles as understood within modernity as "a kind of punctual hole blown in the regular order of things from outside, that is, from the transcendent."[38] This is part of how a focus on the "immanent frame" has affected preaching.

As awareness of transcendence has waned, the immanent frame of existence has swelled and with it comes an enhanced view of human agency in our world. Preachers certainly don't deny God's existence but, in many contexts, preaching tends to focus

36. Taylor, *Secular Age*, 544.
37. Taylor, *Secular Age*, 544.
38. Taylor, *Secular Age*, 547.

on people—biblical people and people today. In some settings this focus on people is coupled with a call to action. Because the transcendent sphere is so marginal and our focus is on life here and now, preachers elevate human potential to meet human need. This quote from Theresa of Avila is a favorite among many students for ending sermons:

> Christ has no body now but yours. No hands, no feet on earth but yours. Yours are the eyes through which he looks compassion on this world. Yours are the feet with which he walks to do good. Yours are the hands through which he blesses all the world. Yours are the hands, yours are the feet, yours are the eyes, you are his body. Christ has no body now on earth but yours.[39]

This is partly true as Christ's body is the church, but when used with a primarily humanistic framework to end a sermon, it doesn't always feel like good news. Rather, it seems to fit Paul Wilson's definition of trouble in the sermon as that which "puts the burden on humanity to do something or be something they are unable to do on their own."[40]

The Rise of Exclusive Humanism

Taylor describes two "anthropocentric shifts" that led to the possibility of exclusive humanism. The first involves a focus on discipline and holy living that was associated with renewal in Western Christianity.[41] Christianity ordered life in medieval Christendom, but in Taylor's words, people lived their faith at different "speeds."[42] There could be quite a gap between a monk on one end and a field laborer on the other. Read through Taylor's lenses, the Reformation sought to level life, collapsing distance between sacred and profane. Ordinary people were expected to live out their Christian

39. *Sing the Journey*, 164.
40. Wilson, *Four Pages*, 24.
41. Taylor, *Secular Age*, 244.
42. Taylor, *Secular Age*, 62.

vocations for the glory of God.[43] This means living into the paradox to be "in the world" but not "of the world." Everyone now needs to satisfy all the demands of the gospel *and* effectively live out their various vocations.[44] This is the oft-repeated tenet of Protestantism, "the priesthood of all believers."

As the spotlight focused on how Christians were called to live in light of the gospel, God as a primary actor receded into the shadows. Believers inadvertently began to exchange "something secondary for the primary goal of centering everything on God."[45] The second shift is related. Without a sense of the ultimate, the arena of focus becomes purely human—purely creaturely flourishing. This goal seems attainable, and it becomes difficult to understand what grace is and why it is essential.[46]

A light humanism is present in many congregations—a derivation of the exclusive humanism Taylor discusses. We profess belief in God but may live or preach as if God is not actively at work in our world. Preaching in this vein may fail to build up a need for God or, if a need is expressed, it will be met with a call for human action.

Difficult to Preach about Sin

With a focus on human potential, human fallenness or sin is often neglected or focused inwardly in a highly personal or therapeutic approach. Preaching trouble—naming human sin clearly—may show us the clearest path for getting to God in a humanist context. Wilson makes a strong case for preaching about trouble:

> The status quo is insufficient; the world is fallen. Trouble is in us and we are in trouble. In God's sight, we stand guilty, yet we easily block this out. We need to be convicted of our own sin, convinced that our ways are often

43. Smith, *How (Not) to Be Secular,* 37.
44. Smith, *How (Not) to Be Secular,* 38.
45. Taylor, *Secular Age,* 244.
46. Taylor, *Secular Age,* 244.

death, shown that we abuse our freedom, persuaded of
our broken social systems, unmasked of our pretensions
to love others, and known in the depth of our no-saying
to God.[47]

Edward Farley describes a "dualism" between individual and
social understandings of sin that has a significant effect on preaching in my suburban context.[48] By and large, most evangelical and
mainline Protestants in North America have a very individualistic
understanding of sin. For evangelicals, the most critical elements
in religion are a person's "piety, morality, felt responses, and destiny" with social contexts helpful as they enable these.[49] Moreover,
society is largely viewed as being transformed by individual acts
of piety.[50] So sin is that which tempts individuals to stray from a
righteous path.[51]

Suburban mainline Protestants like my church are also
viewed as individualistic by Farley. The approach here is therapeutic. The tools and language of religion are aimed toward helping
people feel better and deal with life's "stresses and strains."[52] So sin
would be that which makes us feel stressed, inadequate, anxious,
or depressed.

Farley locates social understandings of sin mainly in seminaries, mainline denominational leadership, and the Black church.
A social approach views groups as vehicles for social change/transformation and sees sin as largely present within "isms" that exceed
any particular person's control. Climate change would be an example of collective human sin. An individual recycling or biking
rather than driving makes little difference but sweeping laws and
regulations can bring change.

Having an exclusively individualist approach to sin is a sign
of secularism. It grants individuals autonomous power. It says that

47. Wilson, *Four Pages,* 112.
48. Farley, *Practicing Gospel,* 60.
49. Farley, *Practicing Gospel,* 60.
50. Farley, *Practicing Gospel,* 60.
51. Farley, *Practicing Gospel,* 60.
52. Farley, *Practicing Gospel,* 60.

a poor person can pull herself out of poverty. It fails to recognize the role of social relationships and "isms" that can wield immense power in our world.[53]

When preaching about sin, it may be beneficial to mention social sin, but the bigger connection in my neighborhood lies with a more therapeutic sense of individual experiences of sin. A challenge for preachers is to avoid reducing the gospel to therapy.

Possibilities

Speak to the Needs of Listeners

Preaching in a disenchanted world means giving attention to the thought processes and experiences of listeners. Secular listeners come to church but are in relationship with those who hold a range of beliefs. They are used to negotiating diversity by keeping belief private. Secular listeners are "buffered selves"; they are largely closed off from the influence of spiritual forces, whether they be divine or demonic in nature. The imagination may serve as an avenue to help "buffered" listeners "get to God."

The New Homiletic was forged as part of dynamic engagement with preaching in postmodern and secular contexts and involved a turn toward the needs of listeners in preaching, including involving the imaginations of listeners as active agents in the preaching moment. Many of the shifts that have happened in approaches to preaching since the 1950s have been concerned with engaging the listener. Casting preaching as an event where the text is immediately relevant in the present allows listeners to experience the gospel for themselves rather than relying mainly on evidence presented by the preacher.[54]

Narrative was emphasized as a powerful tool for structuring the whole sermon and for inviting listeners to participate in meaning-making.[55] People make sense of their lives and experi-

53. Farley, *Practicing Gospel*, 59.
54. Wilson, *Four Pages*, 7–9.
55. Wilson, *Four Pages*, 9–10.

ences through story. I've often watched my own children engage in narrative play where they process something that happened in the day. Sharing a personal story in a sermon can create a sense of relational connection or perceived intimacy. My own recent work on preaching and trauma names story as an important way in which preachers can show care and sensitivity that can nurture resilience. For example, if a story may be sensitive to listeners, I have advocated for preachers to offer trigger warnings, which restores agency to survivors and acknowledges the autonomy of listeners.[56]

Because our disenchanted age is also an age with contested sources of authority, the preacher's voice joins many others in vying to engage with listeners. Preachers today are faced with navigating a fine balance. Speaking to listeners who desperately long for good news and moral instruction amidst competing voices involves creating sermons that open up a space where listeners can make choices and where there is enough creative flexibility for Christ to meet listeners in their need. Narrative is a potent tool for experiential encounter. But the good news also needs to be spoken plainly. Speaking God's promises as direct address can help facilitate an experience of God meeting us in the sermon.

Preach God as Active in the Immanent Frame

Humanity's shift from a default setting of belief in God to the possibility of meaning-making apart from God, what Taylor calls exclusive humanism, has meant that our world has become infused with a greater sense of meaning, a shift from hope that lies in the glories of transcendence to a hope that lies mainly in a transformed world. We see this reflected in preaching that focuses on this world—that calls us to hope and ethical choices based on greater good being done by people here and now.

The heart of this book involves encouragement and empowerment of sermons that "get to God." Homiletically we don't need to bifurcate the actions of God into transcendence vs. immanence.

---

56. Sancken, *Words That Heal*, 66.

Our triune God rules heaven and earth. We can preach both. By talking about God working through people, as active in this immanent frame, we open pathways to transcendence. To return to the earlier example of preaching on the Gerasene demoniac, a sermon that focuses first on Jesus' healing without needing to define whether the man suffers from possession or mental illness leaves space for both possibilities. Application to our world could focus on Jesus' healing work today through people who seek to alleviate suffering and isolation on a number of fronts. One could envision talking about a program for visiting shut-ins or people who have sought to bridge systemic discrimination to build relational and structural healing. The preacher could tell the story of churches who stood with those suffering from AIDS in the 1980s, for example, Antioch Baptist Church in Cleveland, Ohio.

Preaching that seeks to facilitate an encounter with Jesus in a sense brings Jesus into our immanent frame. This approach is common in preaching that seeks to convict listeners so that they might respond to an invitation to accept or renew faith. Such preaching is rare in my neighborhood, but preaching can still foster intimate connection by putting words of grace and care in the mouth of Jesus. To carry on with our example of the Gerasene demoniac, preachers might say, "Jesus says to you today, 'I see you. I see your pain, your isolation, your loneliness and suffering. I am stronger than any illness or pain that is holding you back. I have overcome the 'legion' that threaten you. My love restores you to life.'"

Preach the Cross

Preaching that is anchored in the cross and resurrection of Jesus Christ moves deeper than therapeutic balms and provides a deep and ultimate sense of "getting to God." Preaching the cross and resurrection is not an easy path as the apostle Paul aptly professed to the Corinthians: "We preach Christ crucified, which is a scandal to Jews and foolishness to Gentiles."[57] The cross and resurrection

57. 1 Cor 1:23.

has the theological effect of silencing our clambering. Without the presence of God with us, human actions and ventures veer toward the cross and death; only God can bring resurrection from death. Preaching the cross and resurrection are part of the treasure of the church and fuel the engine of the Christian imagination toward our calling as witnesses. Primarily therapeutic approaches, on the other hand, can dull our souls and reduce the goodness and richness of the gospel to a feeling.

Christ's death and resurrection save us in the vulnerability of the present, making an ultimate "claim" on us.[58] Preaching that is anchored to the cross and resurrection "gets to God" by exposing reality as rendered by Christ.[59] Preachers can "get to God" by way of the cross and resurrection by standing in the text at hand and turning toward the cross or by asking how the cross and resurrection might impact or resonate with the interpretation and stories used in the sermon.[60] I generally move to the cross when moving to the sections of the sermon that focus primarily on grace and God's action. In my preaching this tends to happen as I transition from proclaiming grace in the biblical text to naming grace/God in our world.

Sermon Case Study

This sermon was preached at Fairmont Presbyterian Church in Kettering, Ohio, on the Sunday observance of All Saints' Day, November 3, 2019.

Title: "Do-Gooders"

Text: Rev 21:1–6a

Theme: God transforms us for life in new creation.

Doctrine: Sanctification

Need: How can we live in a broken world?

58. Lose, *Confessing Jesus Christ*, 205–6, 215, 221.

59. Kay, *Preaching and Theology*, 121–22.

60. Wilson, *Four Pages*, 41, 181, 223.

Image: Saints

Mission: Join the company of God's saints in new creation

Structure: Four-Page Sermon, 1, 2, 3, 4.

When Sue and Hector Badeau married, they made a plan to have two biological children and adopt two children. Sue had been deeply affected by reading a book about adoption as a young teenager. By their mid-twenties they had carried through on their plan and thought their family was complete . . . only they kept thinking about all the other kids.

Larissa MacFarquhar's recent book *Strangers Drowning* offers stories and insight into the lives of extreme altruists. She calls them "do-gooders" to capture our mixed feelings about saintly people who inspire us but also make us feel uncomfortable or even guilty for not doing more in the world.

From the Badeaus' perspective:

> There were so many children who for a range of reasons were unlikely to be adopted. These children were too old, too violent, too traumatized, unable to walk, were seriously ill and close to death, the wrong color, or had too many brothers and sisters. They already had lives that were unimaginably hard in the foster-care system. And when Hector and Sue thought about what those children's lives would be like without parents, they could not bear it.[61]

This sense of conviction eventually led them to adopt twenty children classified as having special needs. Sue and Hector were "always exhausted and always broke, and they seldom had any time alone, but they knew that they were needed: they could give love and food and shelter to children who needed those things and who loved them back."[62]

Our broken world certainly provides a fertile field for do-gooders like Hector and Sue to go to work. In the face of tremendous need, these people act. They help others. They change lives

61. MacFarquhar, "Children of Strangers."
62. MacFarquhar, "Children of Strangers."

for the better. Seeing the actions of those who undertake great risk or personal loss for the sake of others lifts the rest of us out of the muck of our lives and orients us toward what is possible, perhaps even toward the "new earth" we hear about in today's text.

Seeing the good that is possible and the brokenness that inspires it speaks to the truth of the human existence. We are caught between heaven and earth. On All Saints' Day, we may wonder, are these do-gooder saints? Maybe. But as Christians, we don't automatically link good deeds to sainthood. For Christians, God is the one who creates saints. The good that Christians do isn't really about us. It is a testimony to the transformative power of Christ's death and resurrection in action in our world. And God is transforming all of us for life in God's new creation. This is how Christians understand what it means for human actions and lives to become holy instruments of God—we call it sanctification.

In Jesus, God bridges the gap between heaven and earth. Jesus comes down from heaven to earth and takes the dirt of human existence and transforms it with Holy Breath. God is in the business of transforming us so that we can leave old patterns behind and start living in a new way that reflects the life of Jesus. Our world can start to reflect something new: the realm of God.

In our text today, John is writing about this process, about the end of old creation and the dawning of something new. While the end of the world may conjure fearful images for us, the end of present reality likely would have felt like good news for the early church. Members of the early church are bogged down in old creation—some are experiencing exclusion and absolute marginalization at the hands of imperial Rome. Their lives don't matter. Their suffering doesn't matter. Their deaths don't even matter.

In John's time, Christians experienced social and economic discrimination. They were poor outsiders who often felt powerless to affect their present situation positively. Even the world around them felt somewhat unstable as the empire struggled with internal and external conflict. As a minority perched on the ideological outskirts of empire, the Christians John was writing to knew something of the hardship, mourning, and pain named in our text.

Life in the religiously diverse environment of the churches of Asia meant that they needed to constantly discern how to be Christian in a hostile context. They needed to decide how much or if they needed to compromise or capitulate to prevailing religious practices in order to survive.

They had to prayerfully weigh when those practices might cross over into idolatry—perhaps not loving another deity more than God but loving their own livelihood or well-being too much to risk everything.

Like other writers to the early church, John doesn't consider saints to be mainly some unworldly reality but rather believers trying to sort out these tough matters of belief and behavior. Saints are people like us, caught between heaven and earth, being forged by the transforming power of Christ. Saints live in a new creation way—even in the midst of old creation.

In the apocalyptic worldview of Revelation, the powers of earth are the realm of old creation that appears to be in control. The powers of heaven are the deeper transcendent forces that ultimately move beyond the grasp of old creation.[63] While the earth may be the place where powerful oppressors rule, heaven is a place where "poor, persecuted, and excluded" people are united with saints from all time and all who live righteous lives.[64]

The book of Revelation is written for a complicated world. A world caught between heaven and earth. It is written to encourage those who are already suffering for their faith and to perhaps reconvict those who may be making too many compromises in their beliefs.[65]

The realities of a complicated world are familiar to us too. We too are caught between heaven and earth, caught between life dictated by the muck of old creation and becoming the saints that God is calling us to be.

Imagine this: you are on a plane, settling back into your cramped coach seat. It's hot. Your neighbor is using your armrest.

63. Richard, *Apocalypse*, 25.
64. Richard, *Apocalypse*, 25.
65. González and González, *Revelation*, 5.

You close your eyes and as the flight attendant runs through safety instructions you begin to hear it. Faint at first and growing louder, the baby's wails echo throughout the small cabin. This scenario can cause white-hot rage in some passengers. I may or may not know from experience that most parents flying with fussy young children avoid eye contact with others. We know people hate sharing a plane with us. But a recent news report went viral that instead of shooting angry glares or making a mean comment, a man seated beside a mother traveling alone with a fussy toddler actually offered to help.[66] He walked the child up and down the aisle to calm the child and encouraged the harried mother to rest.

This is hardly a case of extreme altruism and shouldn't really qualify as news. But I think it says something about our world when a news story about someone being nice to a crying baby goes viral. What is says is that old creation is weighing us down. The weight of life in old creation has nurtured really low expectations of others and us.

There may be something comforting about separating ourselves from do-gooders and what can feel like an obligation toward saintly existence in this broken world. It's not like do-gooders get some kind of "get out of jail free" card when it comes to experiences of suffering and death that are part of life in old creation. Even extreme altruists struggle. What hope is there for the rest of us?

The Badeaus' adoption journey included adopting three children with terminal illnesses. They nurtured and loved them through childhood until their premature deaths in their early twenties. Most of the girls growing up in their household experienced unplanned pregnancies outside of marriage. Some had to drop out of school to care for their babies. Even though they had twenty children of their own, Hector and Sue often took on additional care of these babies. Two of their sons ended up in prison. One of their grown sons molested their sixteen-year-old daughter who had profound mental and physical disabilities. As primary caregiver, Hector struggled with isolation and sadness. He turned

66. Muray, "Stranger soothes baby."

to alcohol for a time as an escape, until an ultimatum from Sue forced him to seek help.[67]

Even these saintly do-gooders struggle in the muck of old creation. We may be tempted to lift them to heavenly heights, but their struggles, pain, and tears are certainly earthbound.

It is here in the midst of our captivity to old creation that Jesus meets us. He meets us as a slaughtered lamb, as one who endured the worst that this world can dish out. But by the power of God, death is defeated and life reigns. The spilled blood of the lamb is a gift of life for us, generative for the birth of new creation.

Today's text fleshes out this new reality. The muck of old creation is actively passing away. And God is creating something new and green and growing in the midst of the old. We don't have to rise up to meet God—God comes down to us. God transforms us and our world for life in new creation.

In these verses, John describes the creation of a new heaven and a new earth. We have come to the "capital E" End and what we find at the End is God.[68] Just as it was at the very beginning of creation. Creation starts and ends with God. God's intimate and personal presence among people brings an end to any separation between us. God will comfort and attend to human need in person. As one preacher friend puts it, "When you love something, you take care of it yourself."[69] And that is just what is going on here. With the arrival of God, the first creation mired in brokenness and death is passing away. It's done. Gone. Yesterday's news.

In the ancient world, the sea is equated with forces of chaos and death. For John, an exile on an island, the destruction of the sea that separated him from his loved ones may have had personal resonance.[70] There is no room for these things in God's new creation. The sea is no more. Illness will be no more. Bullying will be no more. Addiction will be no more. Cancer will be no more.

67. MacFarquhar, *Strangers Drowning*, 255–64.

68. Boring, *Revelation*, 215.

69. Thomas, "Basin, Water Pitcher and a Towel."

70. Boring, *Revelation*, 216; see also González and González, *Revelation*, 137.

Broken promises will be no more. All these things are passing away—and God is not done creating. In the words of one writer, "The sin-ruined creation of Genesis is restored in the sacrifice-renewed creation of Revelation."[71] God is making everything new.

But this new creation is not an easy escape from old creation. New creation is being born in the midst of the old. God has come to earth and the presence of the living God renews and restores, sanctifies it—God makes it holy. As Eugene Peterson puts it, "Heaven is formed out of dirty streets, murderous alleys, adulterous bedrooms, and corrupt courts; hypocritical synagogues and commercialized churches; thieving tax-collectors and traitorous disciples: a city, but now a holy city."[72] God's new creation is present in our world and God is preparing and transforming us for new lives in the holy city of God.

Saints are those who are living new creation lives in the midst of crumbling old creation. Saints are people transformed by God. They have experienced the life-changing power of the crucified and risen Christ, the living God in our midst. These saints, some living, and some having passed on to the heavenly realm, nurture faith in our lives. They reflect the light of God like a planet reflects the light of the sun. Friends and relatives, coaches, teachers, and pastors—these are some of God's saints among us.

Jesse and Edgar are saints, a divorcee and widower married about ten years now and living with their cats in a comfortable suburban house, yet they make tough choices every day to bear witness to God—they are God's saints. Jesse and Edgar volunteer with a program that works with ex-offenders newly released from prison. They meet weekly with parolees, helping them find work, apartments, and groceries. They helped organize alternative worship services to provide a space to learn about Jesus and experience healing, forgiveness, and new life.

Jesse and Edgar are God's saints.

Mr. Bill is a saint. He's been a church youth leader so long that he's been a mentor to more than one generation of some families,

71. Peterson, *Reversed Thunder*, 169.
72. Peterson, *Reversed Thunder*, 174.

and yet the kids still love him. In his seventies now, he is energetic and deeply committed. He goes on service trips, chaperones campus visits to historically Black colleges, and even directed the church's production of *The Wiz*.

Mr. Bill is God's saint.

Ray is a saint, a retired Spanish professor who tutors students at the community college and teaches English to new immigrants at his church in the evenings.

Ray is God's saint.

Adam is a saint, a teenager on the autism spectrum who finds some social settings challenging. He cares about following Jesus and loving his community. He takes a risk, makes calls, and sends text messages to mobilize his friends and church family to rake leaves and clean gutters for some of the older members of the congregation.

Adam is God's saint.

Hillary and Stephanie are saints. Women who have worked tirelessly on behalf of survivors of sexual abuse, they have written articles, maintained websites, advocated with institutions, taught classes, and endured backlash as they urge the church toward embodiment of what it truly means to be a healing space.

Hillary and Stephanie are God's saints.

I could go on and on, our lives are full of God's saints! Sainthood is about God, not our special qualifications.

In a few moments we will be invited to celebrate the sacrament of communion. The Lord's Table is what some people call a "thin place." A place where heaven and earth join, a place where new creation is present in the midst of the old, a place where we take on new identities in Christ through baptism into his death and resurrection, and a place where the saints here on earth join with the saints in the heavenly realm to feast together.

Let us come to the Lord's Table with joy as God transforms ordinary bread and juice into the presence of Christ—a further extension of the transforming power of God, slowly sanctifying us too for life as saints in God's new creation.

3

Preaching at a University
in the American South

LUKE A. POWERY

"Universities are inspiring places, but, being communities of
humans, they cannot guarantee the elimination of all vestiges of
stupidity and intolerance."[1]

—RICHARD BRODHEAD

I HAD NEVER LIVED in the American South until I moved to
Durham, North Carolina, in 2012, to work at Duke University. I
grew up in Miami, Florida, and although it is in the southern United
States, Miami is not "the South." These words—"the South"—spark
images of hospitality and delicious food, but they also carry a
haunted history of racial oppression, though one might argue the
entire United States is founded on this same history. I do not want
to paint "the South" in such a way to let "the North," "the East,"
and "the West" off the hook, because the whole nation has racial

---

1. Brodhead, "Remarks," 216.

underpinnings grounded in a racialized hierarchy of humanity. In 1903, W. E. B. Dubois noted in his book *The Souls of Black Folk* that "the problem of the twentieth century" is "the problem of the color line."[2] This problem predates the twentieth century and perpetuates into the twenty-first all across the country, not just the South.

But I live in the South now and the unique welcome I received in the early months of my stay stirred my attention and reminded me where I was located geographically. I was invited to have lunch with an elderly senior citizen. I saw it as a pastoral visit over a meal and an opportunity to learn from someone who had lived much longer than me. I sat down at the table with him. I blessed the food and we began to eat. It was full of small talk until he made a big move. At that point, I stopped talking and kept eating, thinking, "Is this man really saying this?" This gentleman knew my biography and educational profile. He knew I had received a bachelor's degree from Stanford University, a master of divinity degree at Princeton Theological Seminary, and a doctor of theology degree from Emmanuel College in the University of Toronto. He held Princeton Seminary and Duke University Chapel in high esteem, but what spilled out of his mouth almost made my food spew out.

As we communed, he asked, "Do you think you were accepted into Stanford because of your color?" Then he asked, "What were your SAT scores?" I did not respond but he did with "you probably wouldn't get in today." This was my welcome to the American South as dean of Duke University Chapel and a professor at Duke Divinity School. In fact, I was the first Black dean of the chapel and this man helped me—though I did not need help—to remember that I was Black, a Black man in the South. No educational pedigree could destroy the racialized history of the South and its raced reading of the world.

I was in the South and this good Christian man let me know it. This book is about "getting to God" and in that moment I needed to get to God quick or I was going to get to this man! God helped me that day because God had already gotten to me. God has already gotten to us, which is why we can even talk about getting to

2. Dubois, *Souls of Black Folk*, 275.

God. God gets to us first, even in the American South at a major research university like Duke, where I have served as dean of the university chapel and a divinity professor for nine years. Duke is an academic institution in the American South and that makes a difference. The problem Dubois names is true at Duke and many other institutions. Yet, I have been called to preach the gospel in this elite university in the South. I have been challenged to get to God on campus in word and deed and explore in the following how one gets to God in preaching, in the face of the experience of racism at a major university. Although the problem of the color line, this tortured history of racism, still haunts and hounds our present day as it echoes down the acoustical corridors of human history, there are still other sounds, like the certain sound of the eternal good news of the gospel of God.

Context: Duke

Duke University was founded by devout Methodists and Quakers. Thus it has deep religious roots, like many other institutions of higher learning in the United States. The chief benefactor of Duke University, James B. Duke, walked through a forest with then university president William Preston Few, looking for a site for the new university. He made a specific point to have the university chapel stand at the center of campus. Duke said, "I want the central building to be a . . . church . . . because such an edifice would be bound to have a profound influence on the spiritual life of the young men and women who come here."[3] Among the buildings of West Campus, Duke University Chapel was the first to be planned and the last to be built. The cornerstone was laid on October 22, 1930, and construction continued for the next two years. From its inception, religion, particularly Christianity, was wedded with education, affirming the university's motto, *Eruditio et Religio*, or "Knowledge and Religion."[4] Moreover, the divinity school, also at

---

3. Duke University Chapel, "History & Architecture."
4. See https://library.duke.edu/rubenstein/.

the center of campus adjoined to the chapel, was one of the first schools to be created, and preaching and preachers were highly esteemed. In the "Indenture of Trust" for the university, James B. Duke wrote, "I advise that the courses at this institution be arranged, first, with special reference to the training of preachers, teachers, lawyers and physicians, because these are most in the public eye, and by precept and example can do most to uplift mankind . . ."[5] With this historical backdrop, the life of faith on campus today, even as it becomes more multifaith and diverse across religious traditions, continues to thrive.

But despite this rich religiosity, something else has been present at Duke historically, that is, racism. As former Duke president Richard Brodhead said in his address to the faculty called "Duke and Race" on March 22, 2012, "Racial discrimination was once the official practice of this school, as it was of the surrounding region, and de facto, much of this land."[6] Duke, an American institution, has been infected with the disease of racism, despite its religious roots and thriving religious practice on campus. Religion and racial discrimination have joined forces historically. As one example, North Carolina native James Forbes, the esteemed senior minister emeritus of the Riverside Church of New York City, recalls,

> In 1957, the year before I matriculated at Union Seminary, I had been reminded of that invisible but palpable [color] line. I had applied to Duke Divinity School in Durham, North Carolina. Their letter of rejection explained that they did not accept Negro students, nor did they expect to do so in the foreseeable future. Many years later, when I spoke on Founder's Day at Duke University Chapel, I reminded the community of the letter I had received. My sermon that day was titled "Let's Forgive Our Fathers."[7]

As an institution of the South, Duke was a segregated school and did not admit Blacks at the time. Even the highly regarded

5. See https://trustees.duke.edu/governing-documents/indenture-trust.

6. Brodhead, "Remarks," 131.

7. Forbes, *Whose Gospel?*, 74.

historian, John Hope Franklin, who earned a PhD from Harvard University and who eventually taught at Duke, did research for his classic text *From Slavery to Freedom* at Duke's Perkins Library in the 1940s. Franklin was free to research there but could not teach there. The only available jobs in academia at that time in North Carolina for Black professors were at Black colleges.[8]

One might imagine that in the twenty-first century we have made some racial progress, especially at a global research university that aspires toward diversity, equity, and inclusion as institutional values. Indeed, we are no longer experiencing Jim Crow segregation and certain laws are in place to promote racial equality in society. However, the problem of the color line persists. As Brodhead rightly and truthfully notes, there are at Duke "vestiges of the residual culture of imagined racial superiority."[9] Or, as the Rev. Dr. Martin Luther King Jr. might say about current race relations, it is like Franz Schubert's "Unfinished Symphony"[10] because his dream of racial harmony is unfinished due to racialized vestiges.

The pristine, privileged campus of Duke has not been immune to this racialization in recent years. Over the last nine years, I have seen the existential problem of racism permeate our campus:[11] anti-Semitic acts toward those mourning the loss of those killed in a Pittsburgh synagogue; racial slurs and the N-word plastered on a sign for the Mary Lou Williams Center for Black Culture; and the visible recruitment of students to a white supremacist group (Identity Europa) through stickers posted all over campus. These

8. Brodhead, "Remarks," 132.

9. Brodhead, "Remarks," 133.

10. King, "Meaning of Easter," 446.

11. Despite the ongoing issue of racism and various racialized incidents on campus, I must add that Duke continues to strive to be an inclusive and equitable institution. It aspires to be better. In light of the various incidents, there have been committees formed to assess situations and work toward a brighter future as it relates to race relations on campus. I have served on three: the Task Force on Hate and Bias, the Commission on History and Memory, and currently the Steering Committee for the Center for Truth, Racial Healing, and Transformation. I note this because Duke continues to strive toward a vision of a beloved community.

are just a few public incidents during my tenure.[12] Some of these occurrences caused an anonymous group known as the Duke People of Color Caucus to post: "To all Black students, staff, faculty, and/or Durhamites on campus and in the area: Please take care of yourselves and each other. This campus is not a safe space, and has proven beyond any doubt that it is a hostile environment for any and all Black people."[13]

One blatant, heart-wrenching incident occurred on April 1, 2015. It was April Fool's Day but this was no joke and no laughing matter. Around 2 AM, a rope noose was found hanging in a tree on the Bryan Student Center plaza. The irony was that on the same day, Dr. James Cone, the preeminent Black theologian, was slated to present a lecture entitled "The Cry of Black Blood" at the Divinity School. In his remarks on the steps of Duke Chapel at a community forum of a thousand people on Duke's main quad (now known as the Julian Abele Quad, named after the Black architect of West Campus including the chapel), Brodhead said, "A noose hanging in a tree in a southern state of the United States is a symbol, an allusion to the history of lynching," a "symbol that evokes the whole legacy of racial oppression in the segregated South."[14] As a university, Duke repudiates racism in all its forms, however, as is the case even when it comes to laws, it cannot prevent racist activities from occurring even while working on the creation of a more inclusive, equitable culture.

Beyond racial incidents that occur, racism is structural and systemic, the deep sea in which we all swim. As noted, Duke is an institution of the American South, thus all of the racialized history of the South and the United States is also the history of Duke, even with its religious roots. Historically, Christianity baptized the enslavement of Black peoples and the doctrine of white

12. The infamous 2006 Duke lacrosse scandal was a very public case at Duke and was raced due to the people involved—one Black exotic dancer and three white lacrosse players. For more about that case, see https://today.duke.edu/showcase/lacrosseincident/.

13. https://dukepoccaucus.tumblr.com/post/115190523116/duke-university-april-1st-approximately-1am-to.

14. Brodhead, "Remarks," 217.

racial superiority. An example of this is Duke Chapel, a building completed in 1932. Over the last few years, Duke and Duke Chapel in particular have been caught up in all of the opinions, struggles, and actions over erected Confederate monuments in the United States. Until August 2017, when it was removed, there was a statue of Confederate general Robert E. Lee in the front entrance of the chapel, along with other Southern figures and historical church figures. The backdrop for its removal was the tumult in Charlottesville, Virginia,

> where horrific, racially motivated violence occurred that began when a coalition of white supremacist and neo-Nazi groups held a torchlit march on the campus of the University of Virginia on Friday night, August 11, 2017.
>
> The stated goal was to oppose the planned removal of a statue of Robert E. Lee from a public park in the town. The next day, an individual linked to white supremacist groups drove a car into a crowd of counter-protesters, killing one person and injuring nineteen. Americans responded in outrage and grief, which also served to ignite an urgent national debate on the meaning and relevance of Confederate statues and monuments in our communities today. By Monday evening, the movement had come to Durham: a group of protesters pulled down the statue of a Confederate soldier from a pedestal outside the old Durham County Courthouse. Then the focus turned to Duke, and to a statue that had stood in the portal of Duke Chapel for eighty years, unnoticed or unremarked by many: a carved limestone statue of Robert E. Lee, general of the Confederate Army. Although police presence at the chapel had been increased, the statue was vandalized on Wednesday night—literally defaced with a hammer—prompting an outcry over this destructive act committed against the sacred building of Duke Chapel. By Friday, rumors of a KKK march and rally forced government offices to close in downtown Durham, as city officials feared a clash with counter-protesters. It was in this atmosphere that on Saturday morning, August 19, President Price wrote to the Duke community to announce that he had authorized the removal of the

statue of Robert E. Lee "to ensure the vital safety of students and community members who worship there, and above all to express the deep and abiding values of our university."[15]

For over eighty years, the statue of Robert E. Lee stood at the front entrance of a Christian church. A racialized history of white supremacy was wedded to Christian theology and practice, sending messages about God, worship, and preaching, and who was and was not welcomed. I contend that a statue of Robert E. Lee at the entrance of Duke Chapel was a symbol for how the door into Western Christianity has historically been a racialized ideology of white supremacy. This means that entering through that door was an implicit endorsement and acceptance of colonial racialized ways of being and doing church. The Confederacy, through the image of Lee, was literally wedded to the house of God and the liturgical practices of the congregation, including preaching. Through this perspective, this meant that when you entered the Christian house of worship, it was for the worship of a white Confederate God. This Lee architectural symbolism at the front door of a church is none other than the endorsement of the worship of whiteness, not the worship of God in Jesus Christ, who was a poor, brown-skinned, Middle Eastern migrant, born in a Bethlehem barrio. The church, even at Duke, has been and is complicit in the history of racial discrimination.

This is the space where I preach most Sundays as the first Black dean of the chapel. This racialized history is not only institutional but became personal one Sunday at an 11 AM service. Early in my tenure at Duke, we invited Raphael Warnock to preach at Duke Chapel. Rev. Warnock is the senior pastor of the historic Ebenezer Baptist Church in Atlanta—the church where Daddy King, Dr. King's father, pastored and where Dr. King was nurtured as a child. One of his choirs also came to provide music for the service. This in and of itself was not unusual as Duke Chapel has invited Black preachers as guests throughout its history. It was a spectacular service with wonderful preaching and soulful music. People

15. See https://memoryhistory.duke.edu/report/.

still talk about that service, so overall, it was a so-called success. But it is what I learned after the service that has haunted me and propels me forward in my future work, ministry, and scholarship.

When I arrived at home after the service, my wife told me that my daughter, Moriah, who was twelve years old at the time, asked her a question during the service. She leaned over to her mother and asked her: "Is Daddy going to get fired?" What would make a twelve-year-old girl, after seeing and hearing Blackness in sermon and song, ask this question? "Is Daddy going to get fired?" My initial response to my daughter was, "Well, baby, if I get fired for this, they don't need or want me here."

"Is Daddy going to get fired?" No one had said anything to her as far as I know to make her raise this piercing question. To be honest, it pierced my heart and I thought, "What did I bring my family to?" A predominantly white Christian mainline worshiping congregation rooted in the white Anglo-Saxon Protestant tradition, an academic, elitist, university chapel that is Anglophile—this I knew but I never thought such a question would spill out of the mouth of a twelve-year-old girl, my daughter. Her question has haunted me—"Is Daddy going to get fired?" Was it the soulful gospel sound with its distinct cultural harmonies at a higher volume? Was it the collective darker hues in leadership and an unconscious/conscious awareness of how communal Blackness has historically been viewed as a threat? Was there a sense that an invisible liturgical, theological, cultural, racial-ethnic, denominational fence had been erected, not for dogs, but for difference of any kind? Did she sense the white policing gaze and know that difference and diversity are often demonized and ultimately destroyed, so now Daddy was going to lose his job?

That question is a haunting echo that reverberates in my imagination. "Is Daddy going to get fired?" What this raises for me are the subtle ways racial and ethnic difference and other forms of human variation can be called into question and made to feel invalid or less than, subpar, and worse, subhuman. What made

53

Moriah speak this question? What had she heard or seen or experienced in her young life to say this?[16]

In many ways, this experience and her question, along with the more explicit, blatant accounts of campus racism and a Lee statue greeting visitors at the front door of a church, create some challenges and possibilities for preaching the gospel in this university setting, like many others, where racial discrimination occurs. Brodhead, in his comments after the noose incident, said, "Duke may seem like it's all finished, but we're making this place every day, and we have a choice about what kind of place we're going to make."[17] This is where preaching can come in—to help make a place move closer to the vision of God for the world. Duke is not what it used to be but it is not yet what it ought to be. Preaching, with God's help, can help Duke become what it and we ought to be.

Challenges and Possibilities for Preachers

Challenges

Raced Reality

As in any situation, there are always challenges and opportunities for the preaching moment. It is never cut and dried. In light of the issue of racism at Duke, there are at least three challenges for preaching in this environment. First, it is critical to acknowledge that all of human life, including the practice of preaching, is "raced" already. Race is a historical social construction that has shaped the modern world. It is an inescapable inheritance of the colonial history of the world in which colonizers attempted to subjugate and dominate the racialized other. As Duke sociology professor Eduardo Bonilla-Silva writes, "Racial considerations shade almost

16. This story about my daughter, along with what is written about the Robert E. Lee statue, can also be found in my article, "Do This in Remembrance of Me."

17. Brodhead, "Remarks," 219.

everything in America."[18] From slavery to Reconstruction to the Jim Crow era to the civil rights movement to legalized desegregation, the United States is racialized and there is no escaping it. It is in the air we breathe, wrapping around every system and structure of society. It envelops every institution, academic and ecclesial. It sets the hierarchical standard for what is most important, most intelligent, most theological, most rigorous, even most spiritual. Thus, any preacher attempting to resist racism in the pulpit should acknowledge that he or she is trapped in the very racialized matrix that they are trying to escape. How people hear, see, worship, and listen to sermons, and how preachers read Scripture and embody sermons are all informed by racialized dynamics. This means the very thing one might be trying to preach against is the very thing that shapes the entire preaching event and how (in)effective it might be. Race and racism baptize the world's reality. Toni Morrison argues, "The metaphorical and metaphysical uses of race occupy definitive places in American literature, in the 'national' character."[19] It occupies a definitive place in the church, too.

The Church's Complicity in Racism

This brings me to the second challenge for preaching in this university setting—the church's complicity in the perpetuation of racism. It has been said that the most segregated hour in America is 11 AM Sunday when churches gather.[20] This reality has a history, the unfortunate history of Christianity's baptism of the enslavement of Black peoples and the historical oppression of the other across the world. The image of the Lee statue at the entrance of Duke Chapel depicts this tortured history of racism in the church. In Dr. Martin Luther King Jr.'s 1963 "Letter from the Birmingham Jail," he writes, "In the midst of a mighty struggle to rid our nation of racial and economic injustice, I have heard many ministers say: 'Those are

18. Bonilla-Silva, *Racism without Racists*, 2.

19. Morrison, *Playing in the Dark*, 63.

20. See King, interview on *Meet the Press*.

social issues with which the gospel has no real concerns."[21] The church of that day, or at least some portions of it, did not resist racism in society and did not view resistance to it as part of the gospel. Even today, there are Christians who voice similar sentiments, that preachers should stay out of politics, as if the political realm, meaning society, is off-limits to the gospel and the work of Jesus Christ. There are people in the pews that resist preachers resisting racism because they believe it is not what should happen in Christian pulpits, maybe in lecture halls but not in the pulpit. But this stream of thinking only supports a type of status quo Christianity that basically endorses racism, inside and outside of the church. These status quo Christians may not give "Amens" but "Oh mys" to sermons on racism, thus presenting challenges to moving a community forward in proclaiming against destructive racist powers in the world.

In *Luminous Darkness*, Howard Thurman reminds us that "the Christian institution has been powerless in the presence of the color bar in society. Rather it has reflected the presence of the color bar within its own institutional life."[22] This backdrop creates a challenge to the ministry of preaching because in light of this, what authority does the church, a university chapel, have to speak about racism when the church historically has perpetuated it? Preaching has been used to promote racism and to endorse slavery and racialized hierarchies.[23] Preachers have proclaimed messages antithetical to the inclusive gospel of Jesus Christ, which makes it hard for other preachers to preach against racism due to the mistrust of the church and preachers as it relates to this topic. Why should anyone listen to a preacher speaking against racism in an institution that has promoted it?

Moreover, for a Black preacher in a predominantly white university setting in the South, the racial imagination is fully at

21. http://www.africa.upenn.edu/Articles_Gen/Letter_Birmingham.html.

22. Thurman, *Luminous Darkness*, 105.

23. Even in the homiletics guild, there is an unspoken racialized hierarchy in academic literature. For some insight into this dynamic, see Kim-Cragg, "Homiletical Interdisciplinary Interrogation."

play. As Bonilla-Silva writes, "In this country, racial 'others' of dark complexion are always viewed as incapable of doing much; we are regarded and treated as secondary actors only good for doing beds in hotels or working in fast-food restaurants."[24] It can be a challenge for a person of color to be in a leadership role because this has not been the typical expectation in a racialized world. This is true for a Black man serving as a dean of a university chapel, as the religious figurehead at a major university. What does it mean to be a Black preacher in a predominantly white university context in the South, preaching about racism, against racism? How would one avoid the accusations of playing the "race card" or making everything about race?

Color-Blind Doctrine

This can be particularly challenging and problematic to handle when many people believe in a postracial, color-blind doctrine. This is a third challenge for preaching in this environment. Of course, we are not in Jim Crow racism any longer, with its blatant biological racism and promotion of moral inferiority. Because of this many assume racism no longer exists. One might hear, "We're past that day of racism," thus people do not see the need for talking about it any longer. In this postracial, color-blind imagination, racism is a nonissue, therefore there is no need to discuss it in preaching. There is an underlying imaginary belief that race does not matter anymore and does not impact society or the church.

But there is the notion of "color-blind racism" that "explains contemporary racial inequality as the outcome of nonracial dynamics. . . . Whites rationalize minorities' contemporary status as the product of market dynamics, naturally occurring phenomena, and Blacks' imputed cultural limitations." This racism "otherizes softly"[25] and is more indirect in nature. Yet for those who promote color-blindness, a question might be, "Why even preach about

24. Bonilla-Silva, *Racism without Racists*, ix.

25. Bonilla-Silva, *Racism without Racists*, 3. For brief definitions of the four frames of color-blind racism, see 56–57.

racism or against it?" It is a challenge for preachers to talk about something to those who believe it no longer is a problem or even exists. "Color doesn't matter," some might say. On one level this is true, but it *does* matter because it has shaped how we live today in the world. If we are blind to it, we will be oblivious to the ways that racism still operates in society and the church. If race did not matter, there would have been no need for a senior citizen to tell me that I would not be accepted into Stanford University today. Underneath that comment were racialized ideals of humanity. If race did not matter and influence how we live, the majority of university facilities workers would still not be racialized others— nonwhite Black and brown folks. No one can be color-blind, if we have sight. It is there in our eyes and in the air but not everyone believes that, even those who might be listening to our sermons. There are definitely challenges, but also opportunities for preaching in this university setting. The question is, "What will we do about it through our preaching?" Some homiletical options follow in the subsequent section.

Possibilities

Naming the sin of racism in preaching

When dealing with racism in preaching at a major research university like Duke, it is critical to name the "trouble in the world." As Paul Scott Wilson writes, "Trouble is in us and we are in trouble."[26] The trouble in the world and in human beings is racism. This is the truth and there is no way to get to God if the truth is not named first. The truth will get you to God and set people free. The truth is that there are racialized vestiges lurking all around society, thus it would behoove a preacher not to ignore the obvious but to name the sin of racism at work in society and on campus. Calling it "sin" frames racism as a theological problem in the presence of God. Racism, sin, distances humans from God and one another and it has nothing to do with the fruit of the Spirit. Racism is anti-God,

26. Wilson, *Four Pages*, 111.

thus sin. The sin of racism can be called idolatry, estrangement, bondage, and even more, but naming it as sin is liberating and necessary, especially if and when there is denial of its presence. Placing racism in the category of sin points to it "as more than individual acts" but also social in nature.[27] Preachers have the opportunity to name the hurt endured and caused by racist acts, words, and systems. I would encourage preachers to "name it and claim it" as it relates to this topic. Name the racism and claim it as something real in life, not a façade or make believe. Preachers can, as Charles Campbell teaches, "expose" the powers[28] at play as a way forward to God, hope, and good news.

The trouble needs to be named before we attempt to get to any sort of triumph over trials and tribulations. Name the sin of recruiting students into white supremacists' groups on an "enlightened" university campus. Name the sin of writing racial slurs on posters or buildings to mock or intimidate *the other*. Name the sin of racial ignorance and hate by hanging a noose on campus with all of the horrific history linked to that symbol. Name the ethnic and racial elitism associated with policing others' language spoken in public areas, even classroom settings. One should name the pain of it all because it is true and acknowledge that sometimes preachers have to preach through pain to pain. Racism is a perpetual pain.

Lamenting racism in preaching

Naming the sin of racism is not enough, though it is a constructive starting point. It is a beginning but it should not be an ending. The question is, "What does the preacher do with it in the sermon?" I would suggest that preachers lament racism in sermons. This is more than merely naming it as a reality. Lament says racism is not right and does so in substantive, elongated, passionate, rhetorical ways.[29] It is "an elevated style" that is not detached from the reali-

27. The work of Carolyn Helsel is very helpful in this regard. See *Preaching about Racism*, 69–83.

28. Campbell, *Word before the Powers*.

29. For more on lamentation in preaching, see my book *Spirit Speech*.

ty.[30] It is connected to the Spirit and committed to racism's demise through speech. Lament is both theological and rhetorical. It is a homiletical gesture that says life is not right; in this case, racism is not right, and God will do something about it, God is doing something about it, God will destroy it. Like the psalms of lament, sermonic lament raises questions, gets angry, but does so in the face of God. It trusts God amid racialized realities. It still hopes even while it holds the horror of racism accountable and calls for its ultimate destruction. Lamenting racism makes it clear that one is not accepting it passively or apathetically. Lament may get a preacher in trouble with his or her congregation, but this happens when one speaks the truth.

It is not comfortable to proclaim and may make people uneasy with themselves or the status quo. Some may only want to hear "good news" but it becomes a teaching moment to help others learn that there is bad news before the good news, there is a crucifixion before a resurrection, Good Friday before Easter. This does not mean that people will like lament. Who likes lament? Who likes racism? Who likes confronting human trouble? Preachers do not need to like lament in order to do it. Lament is faithful preaching—faithful to God and Scripture and fitting for a congregation that strives to live out the whole counsel of God, both the joys and the sorrows, the celebrations and the laments.

Lament is a particularly important sermonic voice within the church, especially as the church is implicated in the history of racism. What else can be said when a Robert E. Lee statue stood in the portico of Duke Chapel? Lament fosters discontent with the relationship of racism and Christianity. Lament condemns it. It refuses to give in to the historical apathy of the church and tragic witness to the gospel. Lament actively resists racism and the ways the church plays a part in its flourishing. Lamenting racism in preaching will also recognize the mental and emotional impact racism can have even on children, though it may be subtle and not obvious. More than naming racism, lamenting it makes clear that racism is not right and not of God and has no room on a campus,

---

30. Wilson, *Setting Words on Fire*, 126.

in a church, or in a community. Lament gestures toward a brighter future that God has for God's people on earth.

Celebrating God's goodness as resistance to racism in preaching

Although naming racism as trouble and lamenting racism are necessary practices of homiletical faith and vital for truthful proclamation of the gospel, there is also a form of resistance that can be utilized in the face of racism—that is, celebrating the good news of God in Christ, despite the bad news of sin, in this case, racism. Preachers are called to proclaim the gospel, the good news. Racism is not good news. It is bad news. But to discover ways to preach good news and celebrate God's goodness and life in God are avenues to resisting the evil of racism at work in the world. This is the content of pages three and four in Wilson's four-page grammar. Rather than getting depressed, celebration in preaching may call preachers and listeners to shout! Celebration is discovering beauty amid terror, glory in the midst of gore. When the weight of life presses in, preachers are still called to testify, "When I think of the goodness of Jesus and all he's done for me, my soul cries out halle-lujah, thank God for saving me."[31] Celebration refuses to sit in the school of racism but rises in the school of the Spirit and reaches a rhetorical climax of joy, music, and poetry.

Celebration gets us to God. When one celebrates God, one sings, literally or metaphorically, in the pulpit. Celebration deepens the theological claims of page four. Celebration acknowledges that God is still at work in the world even as racism persists. Celebration says that God has the final word and racism does not. It proclaims that God is present in the middle of pain and he lifts hearers and preachers alike to this reality. Celebration helps us see grace in the world and not just trouble.[32]

31. See https://hymnary.org/text/when_i_think_of_the_goodness_of_jesus.

32. For more about celebration in preaching, see Powery, *Spirit Speech*; Mitchell, *Celebration and Experience*; Thomas, *Never Quit Praisin'*; and Wilson, *Setting Words on Fire*, 210–23.

Just as enslaved Blacks received the gift of laughter and song to endure and resist inhuman slavery,[33] preachers can offer the gift of celebrating God to resist the apparent victory of racism. Celebration keeps the focus on God and this is one way to get to God in sermons. Celebrate the goodness of the Lord in the land of the living. Celebrate life, not death. In the Q&A session after James Cone's lecture on "The Cry of Black Blood" at Duke Divinity School, someone asked Dr. Cone how he could still celebrate in the face of all the historic horror that Blacks have endured. Cone responded, "I'm here."[34]

Cone realized that despite all the terror of racism that Black peoples have suffered, his very presence was a living testimony to God. That he was still alive when his people were not supposed to survive is not only a miracle, but good news to celebrate! Celebration in preaching opens up a different reality amid the reality of racism. The vast trouble is real but so is the grace of God. Hate may be rampant but so is love. Celebration says that hate and racism are not all there is in this life or the life to come. Love will win. God will win. Celebration says God is present and because of God we can press through all of life's harsh circumstances to God's future. Celebration declares God is with us, even when we experience racism, and the confession that God is present, should spring forth celebration in our hearts. Celebration may not be expected in situations of racism but that is because we do not always expect God to be present even though he is with us, always. Preachers can help others see where God is at work.

Calling for reconciliation in preaching

One last possibility for preaching amid racism on a university campus is the clarion call toward reconciliation.[35] This is not a

33. See the story of High John de Conqueror in Hurston, *Sanctified Church*, 69–78.

34. See https://divinity.capture.duke.edu/Panopto/Pages/Viewer.aspx?id=d9a17aed-fff5-44fd-a04b-315b84a871a1.

35. For more about preaching and reconciliation, see Lischer, *End of Words*.

call for cheap community or reconciliation, which is not usually connected with truth-telling and justice-making. But it is an honest acknowledgement that we have a "ministry of reconciliation" (2 Cor 5:18) in the church, a deep calling to form community, a diverse and unified one, as is taught in 1 Corinthians. This homiletical call affirms the baptismal Scripture in Galatians as a foundation—"There is no longer Jew or Greek, there is no longer slave or free, there is no longer male and female; for all of you are one in Christ Jesus" (Gal 3:28). Oneness becomes a value, not divisiveness. It is the embrace of what Dr. King called "the world house," the realization that all people are interconnected with each other and need each other for surviving and thriving. The world house is a "worldwide fellowship that lifts neighborly concern beyond one's tribe, race, class, and nation . . . [as] a call for an all-embracing and unconditional love for all [people]."[36] Preaching reconciliation presents a larger vision of humanity, a new humanity, a new creation, true communion with each other and God, where there are no more walls of division (Eph 2:14). Archbishop Desmond Tutu wrote, "We were made for togetherness."[37] This homiletical approach pushes past the myopic, evil vision of racism and racialized hierarchies that present some races above others rather than seeing the commonality among us all.

In so many ways, this type of preaching moves a community toward the vision of Pentecost, with its unified central focus on God amid multiplicity and diversity through multiple languages and ethnicities. There is the gift of speaking and hearing across cultures. There is no racialized hierarchy but a unity, not uniformity, centered on God. There is particularity and universality held together. Calling for reconciliation does this—it does not erase specificity while focusing our attention on "God's deeds of power" (Acts 2:11). God's community is not homogeneous but heterogeneous. God's community is a beautiful mosaic.

---

36. King, *Where Do We Go from Here?*, 201.

37. Tutu, *In God's Hands*, 34.

The gift of this Pentecost community, of "the world house," is that it is "not a homogenous unity, but a differentiated one."[38] In God's hands the makeup of the church, the nature of the world, is diverse, like it or not. The Spirit is poured out on all flesh, all human beings. It is so important to proclaim that the Spirit is no respecter of persons when it comes to showering power and presence. It embraces what James Forbes calls "the gospel of human race equality of being" rather than "the gospel of racial exceptionalism."[39] This type of preaching can happen only by the power of the Spirit of fellowship.[40] It is an antidote to preaching that wants to ignore racism or preaching that promotes it. It is a kind of preaching that leans into God's future present.

Sermon Case Study

This sermon was preached for Founders' Sunday at Duke Chapel on October 7, 2013, during the celebration of fifty years of integration at the undergraduate level of Duke University. Some of the first Black undergraduates were present for this 11 AM worship service. Liturgically, it was also World Communion Sunday.

Title: Rivers of Memory

Text: Psalm 137

Theme: God re-members us.

Doctrine: Reconciliation

Need: Will we be re-membered?

Image: Rivers

Mission: Seek to re-member the beloved community of God

Structure: Four-Page Sermon, 1, 2, 3, 4

38. Welker, *God the Spirit*, 228.
39. Forbes, *Whose Gospel?*, 69–94.
40. Powery, *Spirit Speech*, 77–89.

Nineteen-sixty-three. What a year. I have no clue where I was. I don't remember. But, remembering is wise so today I want to remember. I do not want to forget. But memory is a tricky thing. We may just forget or suffer from some form of amnesia. Or we may engage in selective memory. Mark Twain once said, "When I was younger, I could remember anything, whether it happened or not." We may choose what to remember and what to forget. If we are honest with ourselves when we remember, we may realize that the things we once did all day long, now take us all day long to do. Our memories may even be distorted and imaginary—sometimes oral history may just be the oral version of his story and not history at all. Recently, someone told me that in his memory, I was six feet nine inches tall (I suppose the Duke Chapel pulpit helped with that) but now he sees that I'm just "tall in the Spirit." I like that but you see how rumors start! We need to remember, but we need to remember rightly in a world that has gone wrong.

Nineteen-sixty-three. What a year. Think about what happened in that year. In April, Martin Luther King Jr. is imprisoned for antisegregation protests in Birmingham, Alabama, and writes his seminal piece that we now call the "Letter from the Birmingham Jail." In May, during civil rights protests in Birmingham, Commissioner of Public Safety Eugene "Bull" Connor uses fire hoses and police dogs on Black demonstrators. In June, in Jackson, Mississippi, Mississippi's NAACP field secretary, thirty-seven-year-old Medgar Evers, is murdered outside his home. In August, in Washington, DC, there is the March on Washington for Jobs and Freedom as Dr. King delivers his famous "I Have a Dream" speech. In September, in Birmingham, Alabama, four young girls—Denise McNair, Cynthia Wesley, Carole Robertson, and Addie Mae Collins—attending Sunday school are killed when a bomb explodes at the Sixteenth Street Baptist Church. In November, President John F. Kennedy is assassinated. Nineteen-sixty-three. And right here at Duke University in that same year, five Black students integrate the undergraduate class for the very first time (Wilhelmina Reuben-Cooke, Mary Mitchell Harris, Gene Kendall, Cassandra Smith Rush, and Nathaniel White Jr.). Three of them are present today, participating in worship. You, too, are founders of a new beginning at Duke University. We salute and honor you and your courage.

They are a living memorial to the struggle for civil rights and human dignity in this country and the world. Their presence calls us to remember. We shouldn't forget the bridge that brought us over. But not everyone wants to remember the past. For some it is still too painful. We would rather celebrate the past, and of course, we celebrate the courage and resilience and faith of the Duke trail-blazers. But if we are honest, not everything in the past should be celebrated. Some things need to be lamented. There have been many rivers to cross and not everyone made it to the other side of the river. Rivers, like the "River Jordan" in many spirituals, can symbolize death. They may also represent all the tears that were shed. As we remember the past, the echoes of our memories remind us how tears were our companions on the way.

The memories may flow and flood our lives like rivers, like "the rivers of Babylon, there we sat down and there we wept when we remembered Zion. On the willows there we hung up our harps. For there our captors asked us for songs and our tormentors asked for mirth." There, the place of memory. Our memories have a place, a location, a situation. Memories are *in situ*, even if we are dislocated and in exile. The psalmist calls our attention to "there." The rivers of Babylon are the famed Tigris and Euphrates Rivers that flowed through ancient Babylon and now flow through contemporary Iraq. In 587 BCE, Jerusalem was burned and its temple destroyed and the ancient people of Israel went into Babylonian exile. It was not the best of times, but the worst of times. A plaintive psalm with mournful refrains. A memory of misery because it was a life without music and if you can't sing, you might as well be dead. There they asked, "How could we sing the Lord's song in a foreign land?" They couldn't, though their tormenters taunted them to live into the "happy slave" motif. This psalm is "shorthand for the agony . . . of producing entertainment from ravagement."[41] They couldn't or wouldn't—"there."

---

41. Perkinson, "Spittin', Cursin', and Outin'," 87.

Their misery leads to thoughts of murder. Memory can be dangerous. The exiled are enraged and have "fantasies of revenge"[42]—"happy shall they be who take your little ones and dash them against the rock!" This is what being "there" can do to one's psyche—those exilic rivers. Certain memories can lead to a desire for retribution, violence for violence, hatred for hatred, only becoming what you hate by perpetuating the logic that maintains oppression. It is honest in that it reveals how violence enacted upon a community can incite a violent impulse in that oppressed community. We see it in our world when people experience their own Babylon and turn to violence. Not rocks but guns, becoming one nation under guns and not God. Yet one should be careful not to be "velvet mouthed," holier than thou, because "it is one thing to talk of the bitter feeling which moved captive Israelites in Babylon, and quite another thing to be captives ourselves under a savage and remorseless power."[43] We can't try to "fix" disturbing portions of Scripture, as some have tried; it is in the Bible and we said "thanks be to God" after it was read. Maybe we said that not to condone the desire for violence, but to acknowledge the truth of it, the truth of our human condition, the truth of how we feel sometimes. It is a "notorious concluding line,"[44] the result of being at those particular rivers, "there."

There we sat down and there we wept. There we hung up our harps. Were you there? "I'll take you there." At the sit-ins at the lunch counters, courthouse, and city hall of Durham. There. In the Allen Building takeover of 1969. There. Seeing burning crosses in front yards. There. Being hosed down in streets like dogs. There. By the rivers of Babylon, USA. There someone wept and remembered Zion, remembered freedom and justice and God. Those rivers, there, bring back a flood of memories. "There" is branded in your own memory perhaps. You probably have your own "there."

But there is the truth. The truth of the past. Of struggle, sorrow, exile. "There" we can tell the truth and if you don't tell the

42. Braxton, "Maafa Service Lectionary Commentary."
43. Spurgeon, *Treasury of David*.
44. Alter, *Book of Psalms*, 211.

truth, you can't truly reconcile. To remember "there" is to remember the truth, the jagged edge of life, that life is not always easy. It's truthful to speak of the rivers of Babylon and how perhaps being Black and wearing Duke blue is representative of a Black and blue experience, a bruised one for some alumni. To remember is to be courageous. It takes courage to remember "there" and then. To remember the pain of exile. It is the honest truth. And we've got to tell the truth and nothing but the truth.

That someone once said that a Black would never preach in Duke Chapel and look at God! In honor of the fiftieth celebration of the first Black undergraduates at Duke, we now have online what we call the Great Black Preachers series, audio recordings of some of the great Black preachers who have stood behind this sacred desk throughout history.

The rivers of memory flow from "there." If you don't acknowledge that you were "there," you won't be able to make sense of here and now because the past shapes the present and the future. "There we wept when we remembered Zion."

The psalmist doesn't recall only the rivers of Babylon but in that memory, he recalls other memories like the memory of Zion. Zion, the place where everything was settled. A cultural, religious, and political home. A refuge. A city of God. We're marching to Zion, beautiful, beautiful Zion. We're marching upward to Zion, that beautiful city of God. In that memory of Zion, they remembered God and God's presence. In remembering God, God's presence is made palpable even in exile. When they remember Zion, they not only think of the past but also remember the future too because not to remember is not to believe that there is a future. To remember the past is to remember the future rightly because you can't right the future if you don't tell the truth about the past. Memory is a fused horizon of the past, present, and future. All of the mentions of remembering in this passage—communal, personal, even theological—are a sign of hope for the future postexile. It is a call to generations to remember our home and homecoming, our return to the future, a future with God. It is a call to remember that there are other "rivers ancient as the world and older than the flow of human blood in human veins,"[45] that "there is a river whose streams make glad the city of God, the holy place where the Most High dwells" (Ps 46:4 NIV) because God is that river.

In remembering Zion, God's home, we remember that God's presence flows like a river and we also remember that we are re-membered by God, not forgotten even if we find ourselves in Babylon. The psalm tells us that "we" and "I" remember, but that God remembers as well. "Remember, O Lord" the psalmist declares. When God remembers, something happens because God has an active memory. Some may ask, where was God during the Babylonian days of segregation. God was "there" re-membering us, putting the broken pieces of humanity back together, making things right, through the civil rights movement. When God re-members, God never leaves us the same way he found us. God is always working to make us whole. This is why God never shuts down on us like the government; he loves us too much. God never sleeps nor slumbers because he is always re-membering, even our past because the future of our past is not closed. Every shut eye ain't asleep and every good-bye ain't gone. God has kept the door of the past open that we may find a future pathway out of it. It is in our memory that we find the seed of hope.

Think about it. If we remember rightly, we may see our future embedded in the very architectural memory of Duke Chapel's past. The chapel is at the heart of the university. The chief architect of this building, and much of West Campus, was a Black architect, Julian Abele. Those in charge of the work were white and many workers were Italian immigrants. The stones of this building are a living memorial of the future God remembers for us. That to make something beautiful like Duke Chapel takes the whole community of God's people working together. Duke Chapel challenges us to re-member our future that was faintly present in the past. The chapel is a sign that God will remember and re-members us daily. The building itself is the memory of our cruciform future and this memory breaks into the present.

45. Hughes, "Negro Speaks of Rivers."

69

This is why we do this in remembrance of Christ. For when we remember, Christ re-members us—our future, our humanity, our community—and puts us back together that we may have communion with each other on this World Communion Sunday. This table of memory bridges the past, present, and future. At this table, we re-member our future as God re-members us at this feast—one bread, one body, one people. This is how God remembers us.

And remember this—the wounds of the crucifixion were not erased by the resurrection. The resurrected body of Christ still bears wounds. That crucified memory is branded on his body so we do not forget the past, we cannot forget the past. Yet through his resurrected broken body, the past is remembered differently, is redeemed and reconciled for the hope of our future, as the fountain filled with blood flows, like life-giving rivers, from Immanuel's veins, reminding us that there is a river in Zion that will never be parched. Reminding us that down by the riverside we can still lay our burdens down. Reminding us that when you go through the rivers, they shall not overwhelm you (Isa 43:2). Reminding us that we can be trees planted by the rivers of waters that brings forth fruit in due season (Ps 1). Reminding us that we can testify, "I've known rivers, ancient, dusky rivers" and "my soul has grown deep like the river"[46] because "out of the heart flows rivers of living water" (John 7:38).

And though life isn't what it ought to be, life ain't what it used to be in 1963. So, we remember in order to re-member 2063. Many of us won't be there. But I remember that God will and his river never runs dry.

---

46. Hughes, "Negro Speaks of Rivers."

4

Preaching in Prison

John Rottman

THE GOSPEL OF JESUS threatens to change the world. In Acts 17:6, a mob in Thessaloniki accuse the believers there of "turning the world upside down." Four years ago, the school where I teach started a fully accredited BA program behind bars in the Richard A. Handlon Correctional Facility in Ionia, Michigan. A five-year-long program with twenty new inmate students—we prayed the program could get off to a roaring start.

On the first day of the program, the lieutenant called the director of our program, Todd Cioffi, over and asked if he could have a word with him. The lieutenant was an ex-Marine, a non-Christian with a brush cut, responsible for security staffing of the entire prison. "Mr. Cioffi," he said, "I just want you to know that I think this program of yours is a complete waste of time. These prisoners are garbage, not worth your effort. Nobody changes, nothing changes. People come in here all the time thinking that they can change this place, and they can't." And then he added, "But I have been ordered to cooperate with you, so I will."

A couple of weeks later the lieutenant asked Todd if he really worked at Calvin College. A few weeks later, he asked if he had a PhD and where it was from. When Todd told him it was from

Princeton, the lieutenant erupted with several expletives. "You could be teaching anywhere. Why waste your time here?" And Todd told him how we believe that people are made in the image of God and God loves them and Christians need to be in prisons because Jesus wants us there.

Handlon Prison, where we started our program, was known among the inmate community as "gladiator school." You had to fight for your place in the pecking order. No one wanted to go to Handlon. But somehow the degree program began to flourish. Violent incidents dropped precipitously. The Monday night church grew from six guys to more than a hundred. Prisoners started a community garden to benefit a women's shelter. A leader dog program (training dogs for the visually impaired) flourished. Vocational programs sprouted.

Two years went by. One day the lieutenant called "Mr. Cioffi" aside. "May I have a word with you?" he asked.

"Sure."

"Do you remember what I said to you when you started here?"

"Yes, I do."

"Well," he said, "I want to apologize. I've been in corrections for twenty-five years. You have changed everything around here. I've never seen anything like this in my whole life."

When the kingdom of God comes with power it can turn the whole world upside down. This is what Paul Wilson would call the "Page Four" power of the gospel.[1] As God's people preach and preaching moves the people to enact the kingdom, God shows up with power. This can happen anywhere, even in a prison.

Context: Prison

When I first visited the Louisiana State Penitentiary, once pegged as the bloodiest prison in the South, finding God was about the last thing I expected. As the largest maximum-security prison in

1. Wilson, *Four Pages.*

North America, most of its six thousand inmates were, as one of the chaplains put it, "famous for something somewhere." Doing time with this horde of god-forsaken men with remarkably violent resumes seemed like the last place one might expect to find God, so why even bother looking? Despite obvious challenges and brokenness, the context of prison has opened up many gifts and opportunities to get to God.

The context from which I write is primarily my experience with the incarcerated church over the last decade. My experience in prison began ten years ago with the first of many visits to the Louisiana State Penitentiary, popularly known as Angola Prison. Over the past twenty-five years it has experienced remarkable transformation, with the introduction of an accredited seminary program, a proliferation of inmate-led churches, and an astonishing drop in violence.

After seeing Angola and returning to Michigan, I began to wonder about the possibility of a ministry preparation program in one of the Michigan prisons, Handlon Prison. God opened doors and one thing led to another. What started seven years ago as a single nonaccredited class culminated several years later in a fully accredited BA degree in faith and community leadership through Calvin University. About the same time a group of six of those first students started a church that has now grown to more than one hundred with a developing inmate leadership. As with Angola, other churches began to flourish and the prison known as "gladiator school," Handlon Correctional Facility, experienced a dramatic drop in violence.

To those who have never been in prison, finding God there might seem like a daunting, even impossible task. A community of murderers, sex offenders, and armed robbers might not seem like a particularly God-rich context. And I suppose if getting to God depended upon a good resume and clean history the task would no doubt be nearly impossible. But in my experience, what happens both in the prison and outside of it is that God gets to us. And preaching that "gets to God" grounds itself in these encounters with God and witnesses to them.

Challenges and Possibilities for Preachers

Challenges

Injustice

Prison communities exemplify all of the injustices that one finds on the outside. And while many inmates have contributed to this web of injustice, sadly, most are also victims of it. Systemic racism has left an unprecedented percentage of African Americans incarcerated.[2] Most sex offenders were themselves victims of sexual abuse. Many grew up in poverty-stricken abusive families with a generational lineage of incarceration. Profoundly broken people often populate prisons.

But the prison system itself too often incubates and even furthers injustice. Low salaries, minimal educational requirements, and grim dangerous working conditions attract custody officers, many of whom would choose to be elsewhere and occasionally are tempted to use their absolute power in vindictive or oppressive ways. Too often prisons offer a dull gray, authoritarian world with restrictive rules and, as one inmate put it, "ten thousand ways to say 'no.'" In addition, the pecking order among inmates often is established through coercion, in a context in which vulnerability and weakness is typically rewarded with exploitation. In many instances, an inmate would never choose to have someone like his "bunkie" as a neighbor on the outside, let alone as someone with whom to share a poorly ventilated six-by-ten cell. But choices in prison are very limited.

Lost Hope

In an era of COVID-19 infection, many of us have learned more about hope. Grandparents hope for the day when they will be able to see their grandchildren, ordinary people hope for a day when they can go out to eat without distancing restrictions, and

---

2. Alexander, *New Jim Crow*.

everyone longs for a vaccine that works. People in prison who are already short on visitors and meaningful outside contacts long for the day when visitors will be let in again and when volunteers will once again offer programs. Hope casts an eye to the future with a longing for welcome change. Everyone's deepest hope is to get out, to be released, to go home.

But for the incarcerated, hope, too, is often in terribly short supply. Mass incarceration stemming from the "war on drugs," long sentences, and a "lock 'em up and throw away the key" attitude work to squeeze hope from those who land in prison. The political cost of the occasional "clemency offer gone bad" and a future with little or no reentry programming for those who do hope to get out, straighten out, and stay out often leave hope inside prison distant and intangible. In the first few years of incarceration, family and friends sometimes keep in touch. As the years go by, faithful visitors grow tired or pass away. As an inmate's years pile up, his or her world often grows smaller and more socially impoverished. At Angola Prison, 90 percent of inmates receive no visitors.

Preaching Cross-Culturally

Preaching cross-culturally in a strangely inaccessible context to broken, emotionally guarded people largely bereft of hope contains all of the challenges of the most difficult preaching contexts, only more so.

Prison has a culture all its own. For example, in an environment where ordinary dollars and cents are contraband, one needs to learn that "soups" (ramen noodles) and "honey buns" are the currency of choice. There is a whole new language to learn. It's not where you live, but where you "lock," and the person in your cell is your "bunkie," not your roommate.

White privilege is always nearby, in the pews or in the pulpit, even if that privilege stands primarily as one massive feature of injustice among many. Class distinctions when coupled with racial difference present different universes to be negotiated between the pulpit and the pew. This is so whether the prison preacher is an inmate pastor or a volunteer from the outside. The challenges are so profound, one might wonder if the gospel even has a fighting chance.

Possibilities

Resurrection Power

Even in this severe context, possibilities for preachers and listeners also abound. One of the gifts that the prison church offers is the opportunity to meet the risen Jesus. In Matthew 25, Jesus signals the possibility of encountering him in prison: "I was in prison and you visited me." At least three times in the book of Acts, Paul notes how he met Jesus personally on the road to Damascus. I always wondered about the emotional quality of the encounter. Another homiletician I knew once said that a personal relationship with Jesus sounds just a little too hot and sweaty for him. Whether one sees a mystical aspect to these encounters or a more pragmatic Holy Spirit-mediated meeting with one who stands in for Jesus, Jesus names the prison context as one of those places to keep a sharp eye out for him, and so too the activity of his heavenly Father. In this prison context, both visitors and incarcerated have confirmed encounters with Jesus and the inbreaking presence of the kingdom of God.

Paul, one of the inmate pastors at Angola Prison, found himself in a small group of visitors that included the late Ruth Graham. Like many who visit prison for the first few times, Ruth was impressed by the dull gray squalor of prison life. Angola, despite its highly publicized changes for the better, is still prison. And most of the maximum-security inmates in Angola will die there. Only about 5 percent ever live outside the prison walls again, once incarcerated. Ninety percent never get a visitor. Almost all of them live in uncomfortable proximity to other inmates, with personal possessions consisting of what can be packed into a one-by-two-by-four–foot metal chest. Prison life is, from most perspectives, bleak, with little hope for respite.

So as Ruth Graham talked with inmate pastor Paul about his life at Angola in light of his life sentence, she could not quite repress empathy on the verge of despair. "Paul," she blurted out, "with only prison life ahead of you in this dreary, dull gray place, how can you hang on to hope?" Paul smiled. "Well, Mrs. Graham," he offered, "as you know, hope is a person, and I have fallen head over heels in love with him."

Displays of resurrection power often accompany the presence of Jesus among the incarcerated. In the North American church outside the razor wire, preachers are sometimes prompted to wonder how much the gospel matters and if preaching ever really changes much of anything. When one is preaching in prison, the power of the risen Jesus there is often unmistakable.

All sorts of remarkable changes within inmates, prison visitors, and prison systems can be identified. Forgiveness, reconciliation, healings, and spiritual transformation are hallmarks of prison preaching. One inmate told me that the only time and place in which he feels completely free is during the Monday evening Celebration Fellowship Church's worship. While the prison is too often a gray, colorless, coercive context of enslavement, God typically uses the church inside to provide an oasis of love, joy, and peace.

These are the sorts of incidents that often result from preaching inside the prison church, but also serve to bear witness when getting to God in the sermon outside the context of the prison congregation.

Christ's Presence Calls and Transforms

Stories of encounters with God in prison provide clues about how we as listeners might join with God in advancing his causes in the world. Prison stories offer clues about how to identify and improvise the parts that God has given us to play as God moves the drama of history toward its eschatological climax.

If you want to witness to the presence of God, prison gives some clues about where to look and listen, and a context for gleaning stories that one might deploy in the sermon to get to God.

Students often complain about how difficult it is to find "page four stories," stories of God's gracious saving action today. The Bible is so chock full of God's activity, but our secular world seems less enchanted. The prison context urges preachers to try going to places of brokenness and need of the sort that Jesus references in Matthew 25. Visiting the sick and lonely, or attending to the hungry and thirsty would be other places to keep a sharp eye out for what God is doing.

The prison context gives reason for trusting the power of Jesus to enact real change as we witness to that power and encourage listeners to trust and act. I met Miguel Velez on my first visit to Angola Prison in 2010. Miguel had recently emerged from twenty-two years of solitary confinement at Angola Prison. I sat next to him at a worship service in the chapel of the main prison on a Tuesday evening in October 2010. We sang praise and worship songs together. I found out that his nickname was Cumbamba, "the Chin," because of his protruding "Dick Tracy" chin. (If I were in prison, I told my wife, they would probably call me El Cumbamba Duo, the double chin.)

Miguel grew up in Colombia. He studied architecture in university, but after graduating had difficulty finding employment. With few opportunities in architecture, Miguel ended up taking an entry-level position in the Medellín drug cartel. Eventually he worked his way up to become one of Pablo Escobar's right-hand men and a trusted assassin for the cartel.

Miguel traveled the world on behalf of Pablo Escobar, who at the time was said to control 80 percent of the cocaine entering the United States. His net worth was estimated at three billion dollars. Miguel told me that he operated all over the world and killed people when needed, the number in triple figures.

Paris, New York, London, Barcelona—Miguel operated worldwide, but then his employment ended abruptly one day in Baton Rouge, Louisiana. Miguel came to Baton Rouge as part of a team of assassins. Their target was Barry Seals, a former CIA operative living in a Salvation Army halfway house. Seals, whose life story came to the big screen a couple of years ago in the movie

American Made, had worked as a pilot in various capacities over the years smuggling drugs into the United States. When he was caught smuggling quaaludes into Florida, he worked out a plea deal to become a CIA informant. Upon learning of his new status with the CIA, Seals's former friends in the cartel were not pleased. Pablo Escobar sent a team of assassins from Colombia, led by Miguel, to eliminate Barry Seals. The assassins procured weapons in Miami and proceeded to Baton Rouge where they dispatched Seals to the next life in a hail of automatic weapon fire.

The team then scattered with plans to return to Colombia. But as news of the assassination broke, Baton Rouge officials closed the airport and immediately caught two of the assassins. Miguel, the leader of the team, hired an aging cabbie for $265 to drive him to Montgomery, Alabama, where he knew people who could get him out of the country.

The plan worked well enough until halfway across Mississippi the taxicab hit a deer. Miguel asked the cabbie to wait with his crippled cab as Miguel walked a short distance to a pay phone, where he hoped to make new travel arrangements. But as Miguel dialed the phone, he heard sirens in the distance. Soon numerous law enforcement officers surrounded Miguel and the cabbie.

With weapons drawn and shotguns leveled, one of the officers shouted at them through a bull horn: "Get down; put your hands behind your backs." Both did as they were told. Miguel told me that the cabbie had no idea what was going on. As the sheriff approached to handcuff him, the cabbie turned his head toward the sheriff and registered his shock: "All we done was hit a f***ing deer."

After the trial Miguel was convicted of first-degree murder and eventually sentenced to life imprisonment in Angola Prison. He spent the next twenty-two years in solitary confinement— twenty-three hours in his cell and one hour by himself in the exercise pen with a guard looking on.

Then after twenty-two years, Miguel asked one of the chaplains for a canvas, brushes, and paint. For some strange reason he apparently had decided to try his hand at painting. And to his keepers' surprise, he started painting religious icons with unaccustomed talent—the hit man turned icon painter, or more technically, icon writer.

Not long before he died, I asked Miguel about his faith. He told me that he grew up Roman Catholic, but as he left his childhood behind, he left his faith behind along with it. It was not until years later, after years in solitary confinement, that he returned to the Catholic faith.

"What happened?" I asked him. He told me, "Well, after many years in solitary, one day I finally got a chance to 'mess somebody up.'" He didn't go into detail and I didn't ask him to elaborate. "What I did," he said, "landed me in 'the hole'"—apparently a punitive place as confining as solitary confinement, but even less hospitable. "As I sat there, I spotted something wedged up near the high ceiling. I climbed up the narrow walls and grabbed what looked like a small book. To my disappointment, it turned out to be a copy of the New Testament. My disappointment turned to fury. I took the thing and tore it apart. Hardly a page was left attached to another page." All of Miguel's anger with God and people came to focus on that small New Testament. Then, he told me, "I calmed down and sat down in the middle of the scraps with the pages of Scripture scattered all around me. I picked up one of them. The page contained the words of Hebrews 11, 'now faith is being sure of what we hope for and certain of what we do not see.' As I read those words God somehow connected with me and I recommitted myself to the Catholic faith. As simple and mysterious as that."

Miguel spent the last several years of his life painting and working to complete a giant fresco that covered the front wall of the new Catholic/ecumenical chapel at the prison. His work was widely featured and even appeared in an issue of *The Atlantic* magazine. Several years before he died, Miguel was diagnosed with lymphoma. He decided not to worry his family with the news or to seek treatment. He died in the Angola Prison Hospice in 2015 at age sixty-six, a witness to the transforming resurrection power of Jesus and ministered to by his inmate pastor and members of his church.

Sometimes what happens in prison provides color and texture to the text. As I got to know Miguel, the violence and ambition in the life of the apostle Paul came a bit more vividly to life. And after seeing how God changed Miguel from a violent opponent of Jesus into one of his passionate followers, I gained greater appreciation for what God had done in the life of the apostle Paul.

Sermons that include stories like that of Miguel on page four teach Jesus' followers to expect his gospel to enact transformation in people and even the world. In prison God uses preaching to change assassins into saints, addicts into disciples, and rapists into believers.

As followers of Jesus function as covenantal partners with God, stories of God's presence and power in prison give us reason to expect and trust that power in other contexts. If God can do what he is doing in prison, perhaps God might do similar things in a secular university context or a disenchanted suburban spiritual wasteland.

Reconciliation

Another possibility for preaching in prison is reconciliation. At the conclusion of Acts 2 and 4, notice the harmony and generosity that believers showed toward each other. Some have wondered if the pictures are unrealistically idyllic. In prison even the Christian community convulses with tensions also felt outside the walls. Racial tensions in communities outside prison usually appear on the inside too, magnified and entrenched.

Some months into the Calvin Prison Initiative, racial fault lines began to appear. As noted earlier, the rate of mass incarceration of young African Americans is wildly disproportionate, as is the prevalence of lower levels of education. Black students accused the program of favoring white students. White students pointed to certain Black students' past associations with the Nation of Islam. Black students pointed out similar associations of white students with white supremacist groups. One group accused the other of fomenting dissension outside of class and the other group made similar counterclaims. A class meeting aired the grievances and the directors pointed out that disagreements, should they escalate, ran the risk of destroying the program or jeopardizing individual participation in it. Hang on to those attitudes and you may end up incarcerated in a very cold place north of the Mackinac Bridge. Of course, simply laying one's prejudices aside is not as simple as choosing to think and then behave differently. Racial alliances inside often determine whether one flourishes and perhaps even survives incarceration. Christian faith, as history too often has shown, is no guarantee that peace and unity will triumph over prejudice and hate.

The semester gave way to the Christmas holiday break, but no one was going home for the holidays. I'll be home for Christmas . . . only in my dreams was the best any of them could do. Aside from the occasional holiday visit, phone calls were the only possible means of connecting with family. Christmas and Christmas Eve were especially high traffic times for prison phone use. Guys lined up early and got assigned numbers for their turn to call home.

Mark, one of the white students, had planned to make his Christmas Eve call home later when the lines were shorter, but then he got word that his elderly mother was dying. Word about Mark's mother hit "prison Twitter" as Mark hurried to the phone room, hoping to talk to his mom one last time. But when he arrived, the lines were twenty-five or thirty prisoners long. Even with the mandatory fifteen-minute maximum in force, every phone looked like a six-hour (or more) wait. Talking to his dying mother plainly looked like an impossibility.

Mark stood for a couple of minutes surveying the room and listening to the cacophony of voices, as he felt lonelier and more despairing than ever. As he turned to leave, another inmate toward the front of the room noticed Mark standing in back. David had been one of the voices in the class complaining about racial injustice among the Calvin students and prison faculty. He was good friends with another student who had been even more outspoken.

As Mark turned, David stepped out of line and moved to the back of the room. He held the number 2 in his hand, second in line to use the phone on Christmas Eve. He probably skipped supper to get it. When he reached Mark, he silently handed him his number. "I heard; call your momma."

Wide-eyed, Mark stepped up to the phone and dialed the number he knew by heart. His brother answered the phone. His brother held the phone to his mother's ear. "It's Mark, Mom," and Mark talked to his mother one last time and she told him that she loved him. As Mark hung up, David stood in the back of the line waiting his turn.

When the lines finally thinned out late into the evening, Mark tried making one more call. "No," his brother told him, "Mom passed away a couple of hours after you called. We were so lucky that you were able to talk to her earlier." Mark was lucky all right, Holy-Spirit-racial-reconciliation-lucky. God behind bars, moving and active, erecting signs of the kingdom. God shows up and getting to God in our sermons then involves testimony to that presence.

New Insights into Interpreting Scripture

God showing up in prison also shapes my reading of texts for preaching. My experiences in prison and with prisoners have impacted and deepened my reading and preaching of the text, particularly the book of Acts. And conversely, the book of Acts has on occasion helped me to understand preaching in prison and listening to prisoners preach.

Acts 3 opens with Peter and John heading up to the temple. Near the temple they run into a man crippled from birth. This guy has arranged to have himself carried to a prime panhandling spot by the Gate Beautiful.[3] As Peter and John approach he asks for money. Most pass him by, but these two followers of Jesus pause. "We don't have money for you, but we do have this," Peter

3. Hardy, *Second Chance Club*, 181.

announces. "In the name of Jesus, walk." And as you remember, as Peter takes him by the right hand, the guy hops to his feet, and dances for joy. The crowd realizes what has happened and is filled with wonder and amazement.

As a present-day reader of the text, I find myself wondering if God ever does anything even remotely similar today. Does God ever show up? I have always hoped to witness some faith healer curing baldness in some public display of spiritual power, but nothing like that ever happened. But then this did.

Charles Colson, founder of Prison Fellowship, enlisted the help of a guy I know named Terry. At the time Terry was a recently retired philanthropist and business owner from the Chicago area. In addition to his financial support, Colson asked Terry to mentor a recently released inmate who was also living in the Chicago area. Terry agreed but, after meeting with his mentee for the first time, realized that he knew little about prisons or prisoners. He had never even been inside a prison, he confessed.

His mentee quickly suggested that the two of them take a trip to the Louisiana State Penitentiary in Angola, where he'd been incarcerated. Throughout the 1960s and 1970s, this largest maximum-security prison in the United States was known as the Alcatraz of the South.

By the time Terry visited Angola in the early 2000s, Angola had changed. In the 1990s, Angola had partnered with New Orleans Baptist Seminary to offer a fully accredited BA program behind the razor wire. As inmates graduated and served the prison as pastors, chaplains, and mentors, the prison began to change. By 2004 Angola had seen the blossoming of vocational and religious programs, and a 75 percent drop in violence. As the kingdom of God arrived with power, the Christian faith was flourishing, and Angola became a much more humane prison.

Still, when Terry arrived for his first visit in 2003, he said that he felt a measure of anxiety of the sort that anyone might feel in visiting a maximum-security prison for the first time. The warden showed Terry the vocational programs and the hospice center, all run by prisoners. He toured the seminary school and met with graduates who were teaching violence prevention programs and GED classes. In the evening he attended one of the numerous worship services led by one of the inmate pastors who had graduated from the seminary.

"I had never been inside a prison before," Terry told me. "There were about two hundred inmates packed into the room as the worship service began and only a single security officer." The inmate pastor began the service by inviting everyone to join in singing a song accompanied by guitars and drums. He then made a few announcements and introduced Terry to the group. After the announcements, the pastor invited the gathered worshippers to join in a "time of prayer." After fielding a number of prayer requests, the inmate pastor asked Terry if there was anything special about which he would like them to pray. After thinking for a minute, Terry told them that there was not anything particularly pressing for him, but he would like them to pray for his daughter. She has a nerve disease in her face called trigeminal nerve disease, that is very painful, he told them, and they added his request to the prayer list.

As the service in the prison continued and just as they were about to begin their time of prayer, a young African American man about halfway back stood up. "I don't want to be rude," he began, "but I think that the Holy Spirit would like us to lay hands on Terry as we pray for his daughter." So, as the congregation looked on, Terry made his way to the center of the congregation. "I found this rather unsettling," he told me. "Here I was surrounded by a sea of inmates in a maximum-security prison."

The young man who made the announcement moved toward Terry, and soon a group of prayer servants laid hands on him and began praying. "I almost found it difficult to stand under the weight," he told me. "They prayed for me, well for my daughter really. Then they stopped and went on with the service." And Terry and his mentee concluded their visit and returned home. Despite all the hoopla, it seemed that nothing happened.

Two weeks later, Terry told me, he was flying back from a business meeting in California. "I ordinarily avoid talking to people on planes," he informed me. "I fly so much that my routine has become a brief hello or better, a nod to the person next to me, and then once we reach altitude, hauling out my laptop and getting to work. On this flight, to my considerable irritation, as I got out my laptop, the woman next to me flopped open a book that intruded a good four inches on to my tray table. I glared at her and glanced down at her book. It was opened to what I recognized as a drawing of the trigeminal nerve."

"I noticed that your book has a drawing of the trigeminal nerve," Terry ventured.

"Yes," she returned. "Are you a physician?"

"No, I have a daughter with trigeminal nerve disease."

"Oh, I'm a physician and my job is traveling around the country educating physicians about trigeminal nerve disease."

As they talked, she asked Terry if he had heard of the promising new drug that they were using with some success to treat the disease—a drug called "Lyrica." No, he had not, and as they landed in Chicago, he thanked her again and called his daughter from the airport.

The next day she called her neurologist to ask about the drug. At the time the accepted treatments for the disease were either a heavy dose of narcotics or severing the nerve. Both options had side effects. Cutting the nerve usually left one side of the face disfigured and sagging, and the narcotic regimen left sufferers living in a bit of a haze with diminished energy. Terry's daughter had chosen the narcotic route.

When she talked to her neurologist, he told her that he had indeed heard of Lyrica and in some cases the drug offered dramatic results. The only problem was that the drug could not be prescribed in conjunction with her narcotics. If she wanted to try the new drug, she would have to be weaned off the narcotics over a three-week period and then begin the new drug trial. In addition, enduring the disease for three weeks without pain medication promised to be excruciating. Before current treatments the disease had acquired the nickname "the suicide disease" because people stricken with it often ended up taking their own lives. "Think about whether you want to put yourself through it," the neurologist cautioned. The next day she called him back and told him that she wanted to give it a try and began the three-week stint to wean herself off the narcotics.

Day one went just fine. The next day was the same, no pain. No pain the whole next week. No pain during week two either, or week three. She reached the end of the narcotic reduction and experienced no pain at all. In fact, she never ended up going on the new drug because she didn't need it.

Needless to say, Terry connected the whole episode to encountering Jesus at Angola Prison. And if Terry was excited both about what God seemed to be doing at Angola before, this strange incident with his daughter fired his enthusiasm for the future.

As Terry sat in my office telling his story, I found myself wondering if Jesus had a hand in healing his daughter. The whole thing had me sitting there in "wonder and amazement" like the crowd in Acts 3. And I couldn't help but notice that in both Acts and Angola, people seem to have met Jesus as they attended to the disenfranchised sort of people mentioned in Matthew 25.

Jesus behind razor wire. Signs of the kingdom. As they say, that stuff will preach.

Sermon Case Study

I preached this sermon first at Ernest Brooks Correctional Facility in Muskegon, Michigan, and a second time in Richard A. Handlon Correctional Facility. The introduction uses what has to be the favorite movie of all time among the incarcerated. The biblical text uses one of the most famous prison passages in Scripture. I actually sing the Psalm setting that appears half on page 1 and later on page 3.

Title: A World-Shaking God

Text: Acts 16:22–34

Theme: God delivers unmistakable signs of his presence and power.

Doctrine: God's Sovereignty

Need: Will God claim and redeem his world?

Image: Earthquake

Mission: Join God in celebrating signs of his kingdom

Structure: Four-Page Sermon, 1, 2, 3, 4

The Shawshank Redemption is at many points a difficult movie to watch. My friends down at Angola Prison act like it's their favorite movie. Everybody has seen it about a hundred times. Perhaps you remember it. Andy, the main character suffers sexual assault, beatings, and brutality in prison. Shawshank does not sugarcoat the harsh possibilities of prison life. But then during the course of the movie the prison warden discovers that Andy has considerable accounting ability. And in light of his skill, the warden takes Andy into his personal service. Always nice to have a tax advisor and financial expert at your disposal. So, the warden takes Andy into his service and along with it provides him with a cushy job in the prison library.

As part of his work Andy receives and processes donations that come into the library from the outside. Mostly books. One day along with the books, someone sends a recording of Mozart's *Marriage of Figaro*. Wonderful music. Despite the prospect of certain retaliation, Andy finds that he cannot keep this treasure to himself. So, at a strategic moment, Andy barricades himself in the prison broadcast room. He turns on the intercom system that the warden regularly uses to frighten and browbeat the prisoners. And as Andy cranks up the volume, the hauntingly beautiful *duetino* "Sull'aria" fills the prison air. A stunning, soprano voice. Everyone stops. Stunned. A hush falls over the entire prison. For a moment beauty unimaginable washes over and transforms the dull gray realities of prison life.

But the warden, as you might remember, is not amused. For a few moments he stands outside the broadcast room ordering Andy to open the door. Stop. But Andy, deaf to his commands, refuses. So, the warden orders a team of guards to batter down the door and carry Andy off to solitary confinement. The music ends and the prison once again descends into its dull gray squalor.

Now our Bible reading for this morning opens in the dull gray squalor of the prison in the ancient city of Caesarea Philippi. Darkness has fallen and Paul and Silas sit together in solitary confinement, legs in stocks. Scant hours before, the two missionaries had been on their way to a prayer meeting. As they walked along, a demonically crazy young woman who'd been stalking them for days shows up again. Paul finally turns around and addresses the demonic, fortune-telling spirit within her. And at Paul's word, the resurrection power of Jesus routs the demon. In the process though, what Paul does also eliminates her ability to predict the future, which infuriates her owners. They drag Paul and Silas before the city magistrates and accuse them of inciting antigovernment unrest. The magistrates order Paul and Silas stripped and beaten, and thrown into prison. There, that ought to teach those traveling Jews to poke their noses into situations where they don't belong.

So, there they sit. Unjustly accused, beaten bloody, and legs in stocks. Here they'd been preaching how Jesus was Lord of the world, savior of the cosmos, every square inch belongs to him. . . . And now it had come to this. Sitting in the inky darkness of this damp prison.

And of all things, Paul suggests that they try to sing. Sing? Well, okay, says Silas unenthusiastically, you start. So, Paul launches into a rendition of Psalm 9 (probably from the old blue hymnal, it was a long time ago): "Wholehearted thanksgiving to Thee I will bring; in praise of thy marvelous deeds I will sing. . . ." You can hear Paul's unremarkable bass belting out the words. And then, Silas joining in with his uncertain tenor. "In Thee I will joy and exultingly cry, Thy Name I will praise, O Jehovah Most High." Two middle-aged Jewish men feeling their way through a duet in a darkened prison far from home in a hostile world. You have to wonder. Jesus is Lord of the whole world; every square inch belongs to him. . . . Really.

Now you might wonder along similar lines when you think about your own singing together week to week in an often-dull gray world. We too proclaim Jesus as Lord of the entire universe, savior of the world. He is Lord of everything in heaven above and the earth below, we say. And yet we too often find ourselves like Paul and Silas, singing from prison. Singing over new stories of renewed violence in Israel, fighting about health care, and thousands of child refugees at our southern border. Singing in a city where young men murder each other in the course of gang rivalry and violence. Struggling to sing in a city of broken families and all too rampant addiction. Struggling to sing in a city where we can't seem to find a way to bring the homeless home. In a world with too few jobs and not enough human kindness. And way too much incarceration. Jesus is Lord, but the world seems so big and broken and corrupt. So untransformed by his power after all these years, whole square miles of it. And it's possible for the church to feel almost imprisoned at times in a world like ours.

And I don't mean to make Celebration Fellowship out to be less than it is. I certainly don't mean to compare the music here to that of a couple of middle-aged Jewish men singing in prison. The music today seems in many ways, way above average, but it still really can't compete with what is out there in the world, like the summer concert down at Meijer Gardens. And political fundraisers at the Amway Grand or Cascade Country Club social gatherings seem so much more significant than Bible studies here in prison or social gatherings with fellow believers. Look at these little bread and grape juice receptions we have here from time to time. Singing in the dark. When you look at the church in contrast to the larger world, you can feel imprisoned by a feeling of hopelessness or insignificance.

As they sit there in that dark prison, the apparent insignificance of Paul and Silas stands in sharp contrast to the power of the city magistrates. Yes, Paul and Silas are singing, but the psalms they sing hardly seem to penetrate the darkness. As Paul still takes the lead they launch into the final stanza of Psalm 9: "Arise, Lord, let sinners not think themselves strong, let people be judged in your presence for wrong. Strike terror within them, O Lord; make them see that nations though pompous, must still bend the knee."

Still dark. But then as the last few words of their song die away; you might not quite believe what happens. An earthquake shakes the prison so hard it breaks chains from the walls and loosens all the doors. Whew.

The earthquake also jars the jailer from his sleep. He rubs his eyes. Through his middle of the night haze, he sees the prison door standing open wide. Fearing dereliction of duty charges, he decides to kill himself. But Paul calls him off. "Don't do it, we are all here." Eyes wide now, perspiration dotting his forehead, the jailer calls for lights. He brings Paul and Silas out, and drops to his knees. "Sirs, what must I do," he says, "to be saved?" Saved by, saved from this earth-shaking God?

So, Paul tells him. "Believe on the Lord Jesus Christ and you will be saved, you and your whole household." And Paul explains who Jesus is and what following Jesus means. And the jailer commits himself to following right then and there. After the jailer's servants clean up Paul and Silas and dress their wounds, the jailer and his whole household are baptized. Probably immersion.

And after that the jailer welcomes Paul and Silas into his house and breaks out a midnight feast. Oil lamps blazing. And as they eat, the Holy Spirit gives them to feel the presence of the risen Jesus deep within and among them. An almost giddy joy at now belonging to the one true God overtakes them. To know that God had made a home for them in what often seems like such a cold, dark world.

And at the end of the meal you know what Paul does? Commentators see overtones of the Lord's Supper in this passage. Picture Paul as he takes one of the loaves of bread and breaks it. And he hands pieces to everyone. "Jesus says, 'this is my body broken for you,'" he tells them. And then a cup of red wine. "This cup stands for our new relationship with God made possible by Jesus' blood." And as they all drink from it, together they drink in the joy of the Holy Spirit that envelops the room.

As we gather here this evening, that same Holy Spirit envelops us with joy in the presence of Jesus. Warm handshakes. Smiles. Ministry together. Do you sense it? And even though these little tokens of Word and Spirit may seem like meager fare, don't be fooled. Like those little pieces of bread and sips of juice we eat and drink from time to time, these tokens point to a future reality. Little samples of the future.

When I was growing up, my mother would sometimes give me a small sample of Sunday dinner. On special occasions she often made Swiss steak, my favorite meat. On such occasions we would come home from church in the morning and the smell of Swiss steak would fill the whole house. Ah, but dinner was at least an hour or so away. Even so, when Mom got home from church one of the first things she would do was to check the meat to make sure it wasn't too done. As she hauled out the big Dutch oven, I would always be hovering nearby. Ah, it's nicely done, she would announce to herself. And that's when I would plead for a small morsel of my favorite meat: "Could you give me a little piece just to try?" I'd ask. And invariably, my mother would take the fork in her hand and break off a nice little sample and hand it to me. And that little foretaste of Sunday dinner always tasted wonderful, but the biggest part of it was how it pointed to what was coming in all its Sunday dinner glory.

So too with those tokens of grace that we receive as we gather in the presence of Jesus as his church. They point back to the creator God who came to earth to be born as a tiny baby. One who came not just to visit our planet, but to launch a rescue mission here. To save us from selfishness, discrimination, addiction, unforgiveness, bitterness, and all of those things that we do to wreck our lives, to wreck the lives of others on this too often dark and broken planet. He came to bring us back into relationship with God and to finally restore to us into an existence so awash with the glory of God that the beauty of it will simply overwhelm us and the whole world.

You see, whatever is good about church, the potlucks, the music, gathering with family and friends, meals together, service projects, unusual acts of generosity, enjoyment of food and drink, lingering embraces in the face of grief, praying together, all of these sorts of things point to God's future. They're samples, foretastes.

All of those fleeting moments of joy and glory point to the day that is coming like an earthquake. To the day when God will make everything that is wrong with the lives of his children and this world right again. And then as Julian of Norwich put it, all will be well, and all manner of things will be well. Little morsels that signal the great heavenly feast and fellowship to which each of us has been invited and for which each of us is being prepared. Good news of great joy. In the name of the Father, the Son, and the Holy Spirit.

5

God Gets to Us

IN HIS LECTURE "THE Work of Local Culture," Wendell Berry
speaks about an old galvanized bucket that hangs along a fencerow
on what was once his grandfather's farm.[1] The bucket has been
hanging there for more than fifty years, collecting bits and pieces
of life, nature's offerings of leaves, seeds, animal droppings, rain
and snow, as well as marks of human engagement—a bit of tar
clings to the bottom of the bucket.[2] Having seen the tar, Berry recalls a story about Black hired hands on the farm using this bucket
to boil eggs, and he remembers the names of those men, their
laughter and toil.[3] The bottom of the bucket is covered with several
inches of rich humus.[4] Earth is being formed in this bucket, which
has also become a metaphor for gathering of story, memory, and
experience. Berry's bucket has become a thin place, a locus of witness to larger forces at work in the mundane unfolding of life and a
place where we experience again the generative power of God that
is beyond us and yet, by grace, knows us, involves us, and loves us.

1. Berry, "Local Culture."
2. Berry, "Local Culture."
3. Berry, "Local Culture."
4. Berry, "Local Culture."

Berry notes that the bucket does passively what human communities must do "actively and thoughtfully."[5] He says, "A human community too must collect leaves and stories and turn them into an account."[6] Sermons can also function like the bucket on Berry's fencerow. Sermons are events that actively, thoughtfully, and prayerfully gather material from Scripture, our lives, and our world and participate in creating a rich, fertile culture that, by the power of God, bears witness to the gospel and may become generative for growing faith in the church.

Our sermonic "buckets" have specific parameters for what we gather, hold, and proclaim in the event of preaching. Alyce McKenzie tells a story of a preaching student as a powerful guide for what belongs in our sermons:

> One of my students whose name was Blanche, came up to me at the break and said, "Dr. McKenzie, how is this for a theme sentence: 'The Resurrection of Jesus Christ radically alters our relationship with God, other people and ourselves.'
>
> "Well," I said, "That's certainly true, but it's awfully general."
>
> "Oh!" she groaned. "You sound just like my mother!" Realizing explanation was needed, she went on,
>
> "I didn't mean to sound rude, Dr. McKenzie, but my mother is in a facility near here. She has a terminal condition. They are keeping her comfortable. I'm going to school full time and serving a three-point charge, but I still go to see her several times a week. But she insists that I come on Saturday night. And that I bring my sermon for the next morning. She has me sit on the edge of her hospital bed and read it to her. She still has enough vanity, which I guess is a good thing, to maintain her long-painted nails, ruby red. When I'm settled, she says, "All right, Blanche, you may begin." So, I read my sermon to her. And whenever I come to a part that isn't illustrated enough for her, or isn't fleshed out, or that she thinks is too abstract, she tap tap taps on the paper with

5. Berry, "Local Culture."
6. Berry, "Local Culture."

one of those long red nails, saying, "Stop right there. I'm
lying here dying, Blanche. What does this mean to me?
Show me, don't just tell me. Flesh it out." So, I'll have to
stop and think of a story or example. When I've met her
expectations, she'll say, "All right, Blanche, I'm satisfied.
You may continue."

So I read on, until the next time, I hear the tap
tap tap of that long red nail and hear her words, "Hold
on now. I'm lying here dying, Blanche. What does this
mean to me? Illustrate. Show me. Give me an example."
And when I do to her satisfaction, she'll say, "All right
Blanche, I'm satisfied. You may continue."

Dr. McKenzie, I love my mother. I do. But with
school and church, I'm just exhausted. Last Saturday
night, after the third tap tap tap, I lost it. I said, "I know
you're lying there dying, Mama, but you are driving me
crazy!"

To which she replied, "Don't you go getting uppity
with me, Blanche. I'm your mama. Besides, I *am* lying
here dying. And I need Jesus, not just ideas![7]

Life is a terminal condition. What we say on Sunday morning
matters. If we and our listeners are "lying here dying," nothing is
more important than communicating the power and presence of
the living God who for us and our broken, dying world is strength,
hope, healing, and salvation. Bearing witness in clear, concrete
ways that show listeners what God is doing in our world is most
important.

Obviously, preachers cannot control the outcome of a sermon
even when showing listeners what God is doing in the world. No
sermon method or approach can force God to show up. However,
we can trust God's faithfulness and God's promises to show up.
The testimony of Scripture and Christian faith bear witness to a
God who doesn't choose representatives who have life all figured
out.[8] Yet God chooses to be "with us" no matter what (Matt 1:23).
In fact, it is in the midst of trouble, struggle, doubt, and brokenness

7. McKenzie, "I'm Lying Here Dying."
8. 1 Cor 1:26–27.

that we often become aware of the patient and powerful love of God getting to us.

Preaching is a vulnerable and purposeful act, an act of trust that unfolds in a relationship between listeners and preachers, all of whom are dying. By the power and presence of the Holy Spirit, we seek to create an honest space that calls our attention to how and where God is getting to us.

This chapter expands our conversation about how God comes to us in the sermon. The following stories and sermon examples offer us glimpses into metaphorical "buckets," whose collections bear witness to God's active presence among us, thin places where we experience God's conviction and love drawing near.

God Getting to Paul Scott Wilson

As students of Paul Scott Wilson, our understanding of what it means to "get to God" is indebted to his work. In his lecture "How Has My Mind Changed," given at his retirement celebration, Wilson spoke of his own early longing for the experience of a "spark" in preaching that engages the whole person, engaging heart as well as mind, and inspiring listeners to growth in life.[9]

Wilson spoke of learning about God's grace from his grandmother in part, through the recounting of an encounter of divine revelation and love that she experienced in a pivotal moment. This event of God's abiding presence in a moment of loss and its retelling continue to sustain.

In Wilson's words:

> As a child, I asked my Grannie Scott how Grandpa Thomas died. She said he was up in his study in the manse working on his sermon, as he did every morning. She had prepared a lunch and when she called him two times and he did not respond she dried her hands on the tea towel and went upstairs to his office. The door was shut and as she put her hand on the doorknob, she distinctly heard a voice, "My grace is sufficient unto thee"

9. Wilson, "How Has My Mind Changed."

(2 Cor 12:9). She said that because she heard what she took to be God's voice, and she was probably convinced because it was the King James Version, she was sustained not just through her grief, but throughout her life as well. She taught me about grace. "My grace is sufficient unto thee." God is gracious. God is kind. God provides for our needs. God is love. As I struggled over the years with improving my own and my students' preaching, it was Grannie's story that kept coming back to me.[10]

Wilson's own experience illustrates the powerful dynamic that energizes the theological grammar that drives his approach to preaching. We experience grace when we experience both our own inability, finitude, and brokenness (trouble) as well as God's action and presence that meets and takes on that trouble in Jesus Christ. God came to Grannie Scott in comfort and strength with death waiting on the other side of the door. Her own weakness was met by God's sustaining strength and presence that overflowed with so much grace that it brought her through not only that crisis and loss, but also stayed with her for her whole life and has continuing power in the life of Wilson and others who hear the witness of this story.

As he learned the language of God's grace from his grandmother, Wilson named Horace Bushnell as an influence in the communication of God's grace. Bushnell, writing in the 1850s, wanted to avoid reducing Jesus to the arena of ethics or the gospel to "an array of legal motives" and human self-determination.[11] Rather, Christ was to be preached as "moral power . . . the power of God unto salvation," the possibilities of which are endless and have to do with "all that He was, did, and expressed in His life and death and resurrection."[12]

Wilson drew on Bushnell to clarify his understanding of the deep purposes of preaching. In his lecture he clarified,

10. Wilson, "How Has My Mind Changed."

11. Wilson, "How Has My Mind Changed." See also Bushnell, "Uses and Ways of Preaching," 526.

12. Bushnell, "Uses and Ways of Preaching," 528.

When we preach about God we preach about a power in people's lives. When we preach about grace, we do not preach about abstract doctrine, we preach about an event of God's action. I came to understand that the purpose of preaching is preaching not to communicate information, important though that is. Preaching must always contain strong teaching, in prose and narrative. Rather, the purpose of the sermon is to preach people into a relationship with Jesus Christ, who is present and alive in our midst.[13]

God Getting to Us: Sermon Examples

God comes to us in many ways in our world, using the contingencies and particularities of our lives, communities, and contexts to meet us with grace, love, strength, and empowering hope. The following examples offer glimpses of the many ways that God can get to us.

God Gets to Us through the Voice of "Others"

Betsy DeVries offers an example of getting to God in what might be considered an unexpected way, through the voice of a Muslim neighbor. She uses a story of experiencing the presence of God that overcame fear in a congregation. She used this story in a sermon entitled, "A Good Report," on Numbers 13:26–33, preached at Neland Avenue Christian Reformed Church (CRC) in Grand Rapids, Michigan, in the spring of 2016. At this time there had been a significant surge in refugees seeking asylum from Syria, and immigration was a "hot button" issue in the US presidential campaign. Further, the CRC denomination was wrestling with questions about how to welcome refugees, given the political climate.

> A few weeks ago, my family and I were visiting a church in rural Ontario, and our visit happened to coincide with the arrival a Syrian refugee family that this church was sponsoring. This congregation of first- and

13. Wilson, "How Has My Mind Changed."

second-generation Dutch immigrant farmers knows something about what it means to arrive in a new country where the customs and language may be unfamiliar, still there was some fear about what it would mean to welcome a Muslim family into their small community.

The husband, Muhammed, stood in front of the church with his wife and two young children to thank the people for all their help. Someone from the church tried to interpret Muhammed's words to the congregation, but it wasn't going well so he tried out his own simple English. "Thank you for your help, we are glad to be here with you. God bless you." I am not exaggerating when I say that the congregation erupted in applause and cheers for the family when they heard this good report come from Muhammed's lips.

In that moment God overcame their fear by giving them a good report. As God leads this rural congregation to welcome refugees and care for those in need, these believers experience a taste of the exceeding goodness of the land. The goodness of the land is life as God intended it to be. For the congregation and the refugee family it includes the blessing of new friendships, the blessing of a wider view of where and how God has worked in the world, the blessing of love, and the blessing of renewed hope. It is hope for a time when the same Spirit that dwells in us will dwell in all the land. The Spirit God gave us does not make us afraid but gives us power and love.[14] It is in this Spirit that believers all over the world have embraced the good report of the hope of the gospel. God opens our eyes to see beyond fear and to trust in this good report: The land before us is exceedingly good. The Lord will lead us. The Lord is with us. Do not be afraid. Thanks be to God. [15]

God's action in overcoming barriers and extending blessing is generous and inspires a response that is also generous and without fear.

14. Cf. 2 Timothy.
15. DeVries, "Good Report."

God Gets to Us through Testimony

When others are moved to witness to God's presence in their lives through testimony, God can also get to us. With permission, we can honor and extend that witness through proclamation. A testimony is a powerful treasure whose dividends multiply as it is shared with others. Those who have experienced God's grace and love extended toward them often desire to share it. In her sermon on Matthew 9, seminarian Sarah VerMerris shares the testimony of a friend fighting a long-term illness.

> Peter recently had a very difficult hospital stay in which he felt an overwhelming sense of hopelessness overtake him.[16] He shared online the prayer that he uttered in the dark in his hospital room, confessing to God his deep sense of fatigue and emptiness. Peter gave me permission to share some of that prayer with you. He says, "How am I supposed to glorify your name when I can't even go to the bathroom by myself? Can't leave this bed by myself. Can't do much of anything except lie here and bleed? I can't even rally myself. I am empty. Poured out. Like a cracked cistern now gathering dust."
>
> But then Peter goes on to share the image God gave him that night as he got honest with God in the quiet of his hospital room. He writes:
>
> "I've had moments of prayer of confession and requests for deliverance that result in the peace that passes understanding as it is described in the New Testament. This wasn't one of those times. But saying those words and confirming my willingness to follow removed a great deal of stress, anxiety, and wondering. And I was granted an image first of my name carved in the Lord's hands (Isa 49:16) and that was quickly replaced by an image of me, in my hospital gown lying as I was, not in the hospital bed or room but in the cupped hands of the Lord right over my inscribed name. It was a powerful image of what was beneath all of this, beyond all the tubes and machines, the fall restrictions and bandages, the exhaustion

16. Name changed to protect privacy.

and questioning. I was being held up by the Lord God Almighty. In his hands."

In Peter's private moment of suffering, God showed up. And the image he gave Peter did not take away his disease. It didn't make everything ok. But it did something vitally important—it gave Peter a picture of God's healing, holding, already-there presence.[17]

Through VerMerris's sermon, the vision God gifted to her friend became a vision that could become a means for God to get to others. The use of testimony with permission extends the presence of God into new places and new ways.

God Gets to Us through the Church

The church is a primary instrument for God's action in the world, too. But churches are made up of people and, inevitably, also illustrate sin and brokenness. When pastors get weary or the church is going through a hard or contentious season, it can become difficult to see God actively working within our own congregation. However, sometimes the power of God breaks through in life-saving ways through the actions of church members, in such a powerful way that we cannot miss the signs.

In his sermon based on Psalm 12, "Why Not Trust God Again?," Frank Thomas offers such an experience, a story of God coming to a member of his church in a time of deep need and loss, through the actions and presence of other believers in the congregation.[18]

A young lady and her husband, with a very young child, both sang in the vast and large sanctuary choir. Right at the beginning of a formal worship service, in the middle of the opening song, the husband had a heart attack.

17. VerMerris, "Untitled Sermon."

18. This story was a true experience at Mississippi Boulevard Christian Church in Memphis, Tennessee, where Thomas served as senior pastor from 1999 to 2013. Thomas considers it "one of the greatest testimonies to the power of God to use community to help heal and restore."

When I got to the hospital, it was confirmed that he had died.

Fast forward two months after the homegoing celebration had been concluded. The now widowed wife stands to sing in a Sunday morning worship service. As the piano and the organ play the song introduction, unprompted and unrehearsed, she tells the congregation about the death of her husband and that she was distraught and wanted to run [her car] into a tree and commit suicide.

She thought about the fact that the baby would have no mother or father and so she emailed the choir members and told them what she was thinking and feeling. In twenty minutes, she received *fifty-two* emails from choir members praying for her and telling her to hold on. The phone started to ring and a group of them left their jobs and went to her house. She said that she did not know what she would have done if not for her church family. She moved in with a church member and church members helped her care for the child.

When she got through, she sang a selection by gospel artist Kurt Carr, entitled "Why Not Trust God Again?"[19] I am not ashamed to say that I cried like a baby that morning. The tears flowed uncontrollably because I had been her pastor and walked with her through the pain to see this great testimony of faith. The Holy Spirit fell on the service and the church cried a river of tears and thanksgiving to God. Every time she said at the end of the song, "I will, I will, I will trust in God again." With every "I will" the weeping, shouts, and praises redounded to God louder and louder.[20]

Furthermore, sometimes a preacher's own experience of being upheld by Christ through the church can serve as a means for God to get to listeners in the sermon. In his sermon on James 5:13–20, pastor Luke Carrig uses a broader event of self-sacrifice in the lighter context of a sporting event as a metaphor to help us understand how God calls and equips the community of faith. This

19. Carr, "Why Not Trust God Again?"

20. Thomas, "Why Not Trust God Again?"

story is followed by an example from Carrig's own life. He shares vulnerably in a way that opens up a means for the church to share in caring for each other, empowered by the Spirit.[21]

> In 2016 the Brownlee brothers made global headlines for all the right reasons. Johnny and Alister Brownlee were competing in the World Triathlon Series in Mexico, representing Great Britain. Johnny was set to win the race with his brother Alister a close second behind him. But when Johnny came to the final turn with the finish line in sight his legs would no longer carry him. He was dazed, exhausted, and physically unable to press on alone, so he fell down.
>
> But when Alister caught up with his brother, he shocked the world by not running past Johnny and winning the race. Alister picked up his little brother, and in doing so lost the chance to win the race as the other racers passed them both. Alister threw his arm around his brother, carrying him the final stretch and pushing him over the finish line. Such a display of sacrifice, loyalty, and compassion shocked a world that likes to go it alone.
>
> I think this is a picture of the interdependency of the community of faith. When our brother in Christ has no more strength to press on, dazed and exhausted by life's trouble, we do not pass him by. We stop and throw an arm around him, helping him on. When our sister in Christ no longer has the legs the run, laid down by struggles with sin, we pick her up and we run with her until she finds her feet again. When anyone of us is beat by struggles with suffering, sickness, or sin, on this race of faith we are running, we do not pass by, we push each other on, by the grace of Jesus in the power of the Spirit. As Christ's people we do not go it alone.
>
> In July of this year my son got a fever. Seemed normal to us. But it lasted for five days, and on the fifth day, it was midnight and the fever was 106 degrees. We drove to the emergency room and before we knew it our boy was being admitted to hospital. Not just that but they began to talk about heart complications and inflamed

21. Carrig, "Going It Alone."

arteries. Suddenly our two-year-old boy was lost in an adult hospital bed receiving more meds than I can remember the names of. And for the first time in my life I didn't know what to pray.

My mind was so clouded with uncertainty and anxiety that I could not put a prayer together. I have sat by the beds of sick people and helped them pray, but in this moment all my resources were exhausted.

But then the texts came in: We are praying for Cohen, Luke. The many calls, "We remembered Cohen and you all in our service today, Luke!" Prayers from Ireland, prayers from Scotland, prayers from Sweden, prayers from Harderwyk, prayers offered out of hope to the God of hope . . .

I realized that its ok that I don't have the focus or the words to pray today, because my brothers and sisters in Jesus Christ are praying for me.

We don't go it alone, friends. Christ has given us his forgiveness and grace, and in his wisdom and mercy has given us each other, [we] who in the power of the Spirit walk this journey of faith together. [22]

God Gets to Us through Historical Figures

Sometimes the story of a historical figure provides a means for God to get to us in the present. Kenyatta Gilbert preached his sermon, "Unseen Hope," on Hebrews 11:1–3; 8–10 in the season of Advent at the 2019 Annual Meeting of the Academy of Homiletics. "Unseen Hope" was preached in a unique context where the predominantly white culture of the academy invited Gilbert to participate in the unmasking action of the gospel to help the academy chart a new path forward.[23]

Toward the end of the sermon, Gilbert shows how God gets to people in such a way that we can live in the midst of the unbearable challenge of "racial intolerance, religious bigotry, and deadly violence, which has triggered in many a crisis of faith," responding

22. Carrig, "Going It Alone."
23. Gilbert, "Unseen Hope."

with hope and action, what he refers to as "Hebrews faith."[24] He uses Harriet Tubman as an example:

> Salvation in Hebrews means using your faith in the way Jesus used his faith as an obedient son, who pioneers and perfects faith—the kind of faith needed in times like these. The terminus of salvation's hope-filled promise, that is, the good news for us in Hebrews, is access to God.
>
> Dorchester County hypersomniac mystic Ariminta Ross marched as many as seventy of God's children out of bondage to freedom, first to Philadelphia but as far as Canada on thirteen mission trips. Ross, aka Harriet Tubman, did not do this with Reformer's faith; she did this with Hebrews faith. Fighting onward because she believed there was nothing she could go through that Jesus had not already fully felt. The Hebrews preacher tells us that we have not an high priest unacquainted with our circumstances (Heb 2:17).
>
> The hope of salvation in Hebrews is verified based on the fact that the self-sacrificial vulnerability and victimization of Jesus was so complete that access to God is made fully possible through the eyes of faith.
>
> *Faith is a way of living based on a way of seeing.*
>
> It's believing in the promises of God even though we don't always see them land. Hear me now, I did not say that faith is a way of living based on what one is seeing. I'm saying that faith is way of living based on a way of seeing.
>
> . . . So, in these times, we mustn't despair. Tough times will either obscure a right seeing of the pioneer and perfecter of our faith or teach us how to face adversity, using our faith as Jesus used his. Even if knowing, to use the words of famed novelist James Baldwin, "not everything faced can be changed, but knowing [for certain] that nothing can be changed until it is faced."[25] We are Christians—preachers and teachers—third eye seers spiritually and intellectually negotiating a moment of ruptured imagination that has triggered in many of us a

---

24. Gilbert, "Book Contribution."
25. Baldwin, "As Much Truth."

crisis of faith. May we be found trusting God in radical obedience, having the same hope as did the company of Scripture's faithful . . .

Assured that our faith will be perfected, unseen hands will support us and our work, and our souls will be secured in a better country—one whose builder and architect is God.[26]

The example of Harriet Tubman was suited to the text and theme of the sermon. The film *Harriet,* based on Tubman's life, had been released a month earlier. The sermon did its job in the opening service for the meetings and papers that followed, offering a path forward fueled by the promise and experience of God getting to us.

God Gets to Us through News Stories

Sometimes we encounter an event in the midst of the twenty-four-hour news cycle that catches us off guard and resonates deeply with who we know God to be from Scripture or theology. These events may not be clearly linked with God in our world, but when we look with our "God-lenses" we can clearly make out "God's divine signature."[27]

In his sermon on Luke 5:1–11, Sam Parkes uses an event of heroic rescue in the sinking of the cruise ship *Costa Concordia* as a metaphor for Jesus' saving action toward us. The sermon was preached at Windermere United Church in Toronto, where Parkes served as guest preacher in 2012, when the cruise ship disaster was in the news cycle.

> They weren't out fishing. Rather, they were trying to enjoy a holiday cruise when the *Costa Concordia* cruise ship ran aground on the Western coast of Italy. Ships seem so solid under our feet until such an accident reminds us that we are still just floating in the deep. The 4,200 passengers were directed to their muster points to

26. Baldwin, "As Much Truth."

27. Wilson, "Lecture on Preaching." See also Sancken, *Words That Heal,* 16.

begin evacuating. As the ship began to list dramatically on its side in the dark, panicked passengers tried to get onto lifeboats that were lashed to the side of the vessel.

One group of passengers panicked even further when they realized they had gone to the wrong level to board the lifeboats and could not figure out how to get to the proper level. They could not reach the lifeboats even though they could clearly see them from the railing. The drop was too far for them to board.

Can you imagine them peering over the side of the rail down to empty boats that could be their salvation and at the same time know that there was no way to get on them? Can you also imagine a nineteen-year-old British cruise ship dancer saying to himself, "I can do this. I can span this gap between what we assume to be possible and something new. I can take this risk. We need a ladder . . . and I can be that ladder." (Did you see that little move there? That risky move? Would this crazy idea work? Would his frame be long enough and sturdy enough to bridge this gap?)

So, James Thomas, this lithe, six-foot, three-inch dancer, with no expertise in the seafaring business, with no developed capacities for emergency assistance, swung himself over the rail and reaching for the lifeboat was able to snag it with a foot to bring it a bit closer. More than a dozen passengers, following Thomas's willingness to take a risk, climbed one after another onto his shoulders and down the length of his long frame to safety in a lifeboat and then on with Thomas to shore.

Does it seem to you like all of the options are exhausted? Like the system is closed? Like the business of life is bankrupt? Does it seem no one wants to hear what you need, or *can* hear what you need? Does it seem like you know all of the variables and that the net that you have is simply not going to produce a viable future? Does it seem like you are all alone in this boat called life and it is slowly going down?

Then, lovely people, I'm here to tell you that there is a net of safety. . . . Even when your little boat heads out into the deepest water . . . where there seems to be no options, out into the murky depths of death, where

everything seems to end, where every boat takes on black
water, even there, a firm hand will grasp your crumbling
deck and shout out, "I can handle you for I died and be-
hold I am alive forevermore! I can handle the weight of
your life! I, the Christ can catch you in my abundant net!
I can take you to safety!"[28]

God Gets to Us in the Midst of Local Tragedy

When a newsworthy disaster or tragedy strikes close to home,
preachers must speak to what has happened or risk implying
that God is not present or engaged with those who are suffering.
Preaching on Jesus calming the storm in Mark 4: 35–41, seminary
student Thomas Andrew addresses the Memorial Day 2019 tornadoes that shook Dayton, Ohio.[29] After showing Jesus' power to still
the storm in the biblical text, Andrew moved to show God stilling
the "storms" in Dayton.

> The violent winds of Memorial Day had barely ceased
> when the Holy Spirit harnessed and mobilized the power
> of love. Tornado damage to those able to afford insur-
> ance was an incredible nuisance, but for those who did
> not have such resources it was devastating. Miami Valley
> Council Scouts were engaged in clean-up and lending
> assistance to their stricken neighbors the very next day.
> Stories abound of Daytonians helping those in need after
> the disaster.
>
> Make no mistake. God is the author of all that is
> good. Anyone doing an act of authentic good, intention-
> ally or not, is inspired and moved by God. Listen, it is the
> same Spirit of God moving through this community to
> calm the storm that calmed the Sea of Galilee through
> Christ.
>
> . . . God's grace surrounds us and is in action in all
> times, in all places, for all people. Our mission is sim-
> ply to trust in his care. He is faithful to be with us—not
> necessarily preventing all, but in and through all. He was

28. Parkes, "Jesus in Your Business."
29. Andrew, "Jesus Stills Our Storms."

in the lion's den with Daniel, in the fiery furnace with
Shadrach, Meshach, and Abednego. He went through the
valley of the shadow of death with David. And He will do
the same for us. Brother Andraé Crouch preached it in
song: "Through it all, through it all. I've learned to trust
in Jesus. I've learned to trust in God."[30]

Andrew provides a means for God to get to listeners through
the link between the storm in the text and the tornado in Dayton.
Utilizing tools that can help preachers address trauma, he honestly
names the situation, speaks about God's power, and quotes from
Scripture to evoke deep language of faith.[31]

In another context, Jerusha Matsen Neal gets her sermon to
God in the devastating aftermath of hurricane Winston, which hit
Fiji in 2016. In her work with Mark 2:1–12, where people remove
a roof to get their paralyzed friend to Jesus, Matsen Neal realized
that the reality faced by her Fijian students with missing or dam-
aged roofs following the hurricane had changed their relationship
with the text. This "trouble" became an opportunity for listeners to
experience the healing power of Christ.

Just like he was in Capernaum all those years ago, Jesus
is in Fiji today, sitting in houses with broken roofs, with
paralyzed, doubting people giving a fresh start. He is
speaking a word of healing to families having devotions
by candlelight in Ra. Speaking words of forgiveness and
peace to those who are afraid that the storm was their
fault. Reminding those paralyzed by weariness and fear
that their days for standing up and walking are not over.

He doesn't offer answers to the question of why.
But he does say this: "So that you know that the Son of
Man has the authority to forgive sins, I say to you Stand.
And Go." And all over this nation, paralyzed people
are rising to their feet. Villages are refusing the drug of
despair. A church is responding with supplies and food,
builders and counselors. Families crowded together in
a home with a hole are realizing the good news of the

---

30. Andrew, "Jesus Stills Our Storms."

31. Sancken, *Words That Heal*, 108–9.

gospel—maybe for the very first time. God is right there with them. And he is doing his very best work.

Do you want to know what *redemption* means? It means this. The God revealed in Jesus can take the most painful events of our lives—the deadliest storm, the greatest loss—and can turn it for good. We will rebuild from cyclone Winston—the holes in the homes of this nation will be repaired. But years from now, when stories are told about this season of struggle, you wait and see. There will be testimonies to the God who does his very best saving work, his very best healing work, in a home with a hole.[32]

Matsen Neal's vivid imaging of redemption and naming Christ's healing and hopeful action in the recovery after cyclone Winston opened a space to bring us into the presence and power of God.

Conclusion

The examples and suggestions offered here represent only a fraction of the ways that God can get to us in sermons. The story of Jesus healing a paralyzed man from Mark 2, highlighted in Jerusha Matsen Neal's sermon, provides a powerful image for God's determination to get to us. Like the roof that is removed to open up a space for a healing encounter, nothing is a barrier for our God. Even death is not a barrier for our God. God's love is nimble, relentless, able to meet us wherever we are, opening up thin places of possibility, hope, conviction, healing, and strength.

We have asserted that the primary destination of a sermon is God. This path relies primarily on the work of the Holy Spirit, but preachers are invited to participate in bearing witness to God's action in our world. Context participates in shaping our experiences of getting to God just as our preaching also contributes to shaping our contexts. Preachers join the whole community of faith as recipients and instruments of God's power and love. Richard Eslinger notes in a sermon on Mark 6:30–34, 53–56:

32. Matsen Neal, "Redemption of Roofs."

Have you noticed that the dividing line between apostle and crowd is never a neat one? Sometimes, or for a part of us, all the time, we come into this assembly as apostles. We have been out in the world engaged in all sorts of apostolic missions—feeding the hungry, healing the sick, and proclaiming the good news. Now, it is time to be gathered and to find a rest-filled place with our Lord. But there is also the possibility that we might be more like the crowd—more like those who need to be fed, needing healing ourselves, and longing for the good news of Jesus Christ. It is likely the case that for most of us, we have come both as apostles and as crowd. Sometimes worn out from serving, and other times needing to receive our Shepherd's tender care.[33]

In the terrain of this book we have laid bare unexpected thin places of encounter: secular suburbia, a university grappling with racism, and prison. Our journey has unfolded in an unprecedented season where the world has been rocked by a global pandemic as well as deep-seated racial injustice. The gospel encounters us here in thin places where God meets us in our finitude and weakness. Preaching sermons that get to God, that is, that speak about God as truly active in our world, are prophetic because they also put into stark relief situations, experiences, and actions that do not align with God's good purposes for creation.

When we are at our most broken, we are sustained by the living God. In our lives and in our preaching, it is often the experiences and stories of trouble that create the soil for growth. Grace is encountering the God who is getting to us as we journey through the hard stuff.

As preachers, we are called to a joyful ministry, to be ever on the lookout for God active in our world. When we look at our contexts through "God lenses," the Holy Spirit often blesses us with a vision of our world as God sees it: beloved, redeemed, just, whole. Consider this vision of her city of Nashville redeemed, offered by seminary student Amy Sigmon in her sermon based on Revelation 21:1–6a.

33. Eslinger, "Homily for the 16th Sunday."

When I hear about a city full of diverse peoples with the gates wide open to everyone, Nashville certainly comes to mind! A hundred people move to Nashville every day, we hear. Almost everyone I know is a transplant here, we are transplants. Clearly, the gates are open! Nashville metro schools have over 100 languages spoken, and 30 percent of their families primarily speak a language other than English in the home. The largest population of Kurds outside of the Middle East lives in Nashville, "Little Kurdistan" is off Nolensville Pike, just across from the zoo. The Nashville Food Project provides garden plots for Bhutanese immigrants to grow crops from their homeland as well as southern staples. We are a city teeming with diversity.

Church, the good news is that the kingdom of heaven isn't a place in the sky. It's our own city, where the city gates are never shut and there is no temple, no church, because God is with the people and the city itself is a place of worship. It's Nashville redeemed, where justice and righteousness prevail. Where God dwells with us so closely that all of life is holy.[34]

The spiritual discipline of getting to God in the sermon can be a profound, life-changing gift. The settings where we preach matter; the people with and to whom we minister, the events of our lives, and all that fills our homiletical "buckets" matter. God's promises are not general news for generic people. God's promises are good news for all people in a variety of contexts. God shows up in and through the lives of real people in real places of brokenness and possibility, revealing that there is still good news in our troubled world.

34. Sigmon, "Rev 21 Sermon."

Bibliography

Achenbach, Joel, and Jason Samenow. "Extreme Weather Has Made Half of America Look like Tornado Alley." *Washington Post*, May 29, 2019. https://www.washingtonpost.com/science/2019/05/29/extreme-weather-has-made-half-america-look-like-tornado-alley/?utm_term=.7413e75e6708.

Alexander, Michelle. *The New Jim Crow: Mass Incarceration in the Age of Colorblindness.* New York: New Press, 2010.

Alter, Robert. *The Book of Psalms: A Translation with Commentary.* New York: W. W. Norton & Company, 2007.

Andrew, Thomas. "Jesus Stills Our Storms." Class Sermon, United Theological Seminary, Dayton, Ohio, January 15, 2020.

Baldwin, James. "As Much Truth as One Can Bear; To Speak Out About the World as It Is, Says James Baldwin, Is the Writer's Job As Much of the Truth as One Can Bear." *New York Times*, January 14, 1962.

Beres, Laura. "Celtic Spirituality: Exploring the fascination across time and place." In *The Routledge Handbook of Religion, Spirituality and Social Work,* edited by Beth R. Crisp, 100–107. London: Routledge, 2017.

Berry, Wendell. "The Work of Local Culture." Lecture, 1988 Iowa Humanities Board. http://www.dailygood.org/story/576/the-work-of-local-culture-wendell-berry/.

Bonilla-Silva, Eduardo. *Racism without Racists: Color-Blind Racism and the Persistence of Racial Inequality in America.* 5th ed. Lanham, MD: Rowman & Littlefield, 2018.

Bosma, Kary. "Supporter Message: Calvin Prison Initiative." Email, March 23, 2020.

Boring, M. Eugene. *Revelation.* Interpretation, a Bible Commentary for Teaching and Preaching. Louisville: John Knox, 1989.

Bradley, Ian C. *Pilgrimage: A Spiritual and Cultural Journey.* Oxford: Lion, 2009.

Braxton, Brad. "Maafa Service Lectionary Commentary." *The African American Lectionary.* Lection for February 17, 2008. http://www.theafricanamericanlectionary.org/PopupLectionaryReading.asp?LRID=10.

Brodhead, Richard H. "Remarks at a Community Forum on a Racial Incident." In *Speaking of Duke: Leading the 21st-Century University*, 216–19. Durham, NC: Duke University Press, 2017.

———. *Speaking of Duke: Leading the 21st-Century University*. Durham, NC: Duke University Press, 2017.

Bushnell, Horace. "The Practical Uses and Ways of Preaching." In *The Vicarious Sacrifice*, vol. 1, 524–52. New York: Charles Scribner's Sons, 1883.

Campbell, Charles. *The Word before the Powers: An Ethic of Preaching*. Louisville: Westminster John Knox, 2002.

Capers, James. "When I think of the goodness of Jesus." In *This Far By Faith: An African American Resource for Worship*, 269. Minneapolis: Augsburg Fortress, 1999.

Carr, Kurt. "Why Not Trust God Again?" One Church Project, November 8, 2014. Video, 6:04. https://www.youtube.com/watch?v=l64BTx-ox_Q&feature=emb_logo.

Carrig, Luke. "Going It Alone." Sermon, Harderwyk Ministries, Holland, Michigan, November 17, 2019.

Chow, Denise. "What's fueling the recent spate of tornados across the U.S.?" May 28, 2019. https://www.nbcnews.com/mach/science/what-s-fueling-spate-recent-tornadoes-across-u-s-ncna1011036.

Cone, James. "2015 Martin Luther King Jr. Lecture." April 1, 2015. Duke University. Video, 1:20:15, https://www.youtube.com/watch?v=ziEGUYKkVGY.

DeVries, Betsy. "A Good Report." Sermon, Neland Avenue Christian Reformed Church, Grand Rapids, Michigan, March 29, 2015.

Dubois, W. E. B. *The Souls of Black Folk*. New York: Penguin, 1969.

Duke PoC Caucus. Duke University, April 1st, approximately 1am. Photograph. Tumblr, April 1, 2015. https://dukepoccaucus.tumblr.com/post/115190523116/duke-university-april-1st-approximately-1am-to.

"Duke University: A Brief Narrative History." Duke University Libraries, September 21, 2020. https://library.duke.edu/rubenstein/uarchives/history/articles/narrative-history.

Duke University Chapel. "History and Architecture." https://chapel.duke.edu/history.

Emory, Frank E., et al. "Report: Commission on Memory and History." Duke University, November 17, 2017. https://memoryhistory.duke.edu/report/.

Eslinger, Richard. "Homily for the 16th Sunday in Ordinary Time. Year B, Mark 6:30–34." The Athenaeum of Ohio Pastoral Preaching website, July 19, 2016.

Farley, Edward. *Practicing Gospel: Unconventional Thoughts on the Church's Ministry*. Louisville: Westminster John Knox, 2003.

Forbes James A., Jr. *Whose Gospel? A Concise Guide to Progressive Protestantism*. New York: New Press, 2010.

Gilbert, Kenyatta. "Book Contribution for *Getting to God* in Honor of Paul Scott Wilson." Unpublished essay, May 6, 2020.

———. "Unseen Hope." Sermon, 54th Annual Meeting of the Academy of Homiletics. New Brunswick, NJ, December 4, 2019.

González, Catherine Gunsalus, and Justo L. González. *Revelation*. Westminster Bible Companion. Louisville: Westminster John Knox, 1997.

Hardy, Jason. *The Second Chance Club*. New York: Simon and Schuster, 2020.

Helsel, Carolyn. *Preaching about Racism: A Guide for Faith Leaders*. St. Louis: Chalice, 2018.

Hughes, Langston. "The Negro Speaks of Rivers." https://www.poetryfoundation. org/poems/44428/the-negro-speaks-of-rivers.

Hunsinger, Deborah van Duesen. *Bearing the Unbearable: Trauma, Gospel, and Pastoral Care*. Grand Rapids: Eerdmans, 2015.

Hurston, Zora Neale. *The Sanctified Church*. Berkeley: Turtle Island, 1983.

"The Indenture of Trust." Duke University Board of Trustees. Duke University, January 18, 2022. https://trustees.duke.edu/governing-documents/in denture-trust.

Jacobsen, Schnasa David. "Going Public with the Means of Grace: A Homiletical Theology of Promise for Word and Sacrament in a Post-Secular Age." *Theology Today* 75.3 (2018) 371–81.

Jacobsen, David Schnasa, and Robert Allen Kelly. *Kairos Preaching: Speaking Gospel to the Situation*. Minneapolis: Fortress, 2009.

Kay, James. *Preaching and Theology*. St. Louis: Chalice, 2007.

Keifert, Patrick. *Welcoming the Stranger: A Public Theology of Worship and Evangelism*. Minneapolis: Fortress, 1992.

Kim-Cragg, Hyeran. "A Homiletical Interdisciplinary Interrogation of Un- masking Whiteness." Conference Paper, Academy of Homiletics, 2019. https://www.homiletics.org/sites/default/files/assets/2019%20AOH%20 Workgroup%20Papers%20Final.pdf.

King, Martin Luther, Jr. "The Meaning of Easter, Sermon Delivered at Ebenezer Baptist Church." In *The Papers of Martin Luther King, Jr. Volume VII: To Save the Soul of America, January 1961–August 1962*, edited by Clayborne Carson, 440–48. Berkeley: University of California Press, 2014.

———. *Meet the Press*. The National Broadcasting Company, April 17, 1960.

———. *The Papers of Martin Luther King, Jr*. Vol. VII. Edited by Clayborne Carson. Berkeley: University of California, 1992.

———. *Letter from the Birmingham Jail*. San Francisco: Harper San Francisco, 1994.

———. *Where Do We Go from Here: Chaos or Community?* The King Legacy Series. Boston: Beacon, 2010.

Lischer, Richard. *The End of Words: The Language of Reconciliation in a Culture of Violence*. Grand Rapids: Eerdmans, 2008.

Londberg, Max. "Memorial Day tornadoes in Ohio set record for most touch- downs in local history." *Cincinnati Enquirer*, May 31, 2019.

"Looking Back at the Duke Lacrosse Case," Duke Office of News and Communications. Duke University, April, 2007. https://today.duke.edu/ showcase/lacrosseincident/.

Lose, David J. *Confessing Jesus Christ: Preaching in a Postmodern World*. Grand Rapids: Eerdmans, 2003.

MacFarquhar, Larissa. "The Children of Strangers." *New Yorker*, July 27, 2015. http:www.newyorker.com/magazine/2015/08/03/the-children-of-strangers.

————. *Strangers Drowning: Impossible Idealism, Drastic Choices, and the Urge to Help*. New York: Penguin, 2016.

Maguire, Brian. "Longing for the Transcendent?" Email to Joni Sancken and pastoral staff at Fairmont Presbyterian Church, Kettering, OH, April 27, 2020.

Matsen Neal, Jerusha. "The Redemption of Roofs." Sermon, Wesley Methodist Church, Suva, Fiji, March, 2016.

McKenzie, Alyce. "I'm Lying Here Dying, Blanche. What Does This Mean to Me?" Unpublished submission for *Getting to God*, June 15, 2020.

Mitchell, Henry H. *Celebration and Experience in Preaching*. Nashville: Abingdon, 1990.

Morrison, Toni. *Playing in the Dark: Whiteness and the Literary Imagination*. The William E. Massey, Sr. Lectures in the History of American Civilization 1990. Cambridge: Harvard University Press, 1992.

Muray, Rheana. "Stranger soothes baby on a plane so pregnant mom can rest." *Today*, November 14, 2016. https://www.today.com/kindness/stranger-soothes-baby-plane-so-pregnant-mom-can-rest-t102693.

National Alliance on Mental Illness. "Mental Health by the Numbers." https://www.nami.org/learn-more/mental-health-by-the-numbers.

Nelson, Greg, and Phill McHugh. "People Need the Lord." In *The Faith We Sing*, 2244. Nashville: Abingdon, 2000.

Parkes, Sam. "Jesus in Your Business." Sermon, Windermere United Church, Toronto, Ontario, 2012.

Perkinson, Jim. "Spittin', Cursin', and Outin': Hip-Hop Apocalypse in the Imperial Necropolis." In *Bible in/and Popular Culture: A Creative Encounter*, edited by Elaine Mary Wainwright and Philip Leroy Culbertson, 81–95. Atlanta: Society of Biblical Literature, 2010.

Peterson, Eugene. *Reversed Thunder: The Revelation of John and the Praying Imagination*. New York: Harper Collins, 1988.

Powery, Luke A. "'Do This In Remembrance of Me': Black Bodies and the Future of Theological Education." *Theology Today* 76.4 (January 2020) 336–47.

————. *Spirit Speech: Lament and Celebration in Preaching*. Nashville: Abingdon, 2009.

Price, Vincent. "The Importance of Inclusion." https://president.duke.edu/2020/03/24/the-importance-of-inclusion/.

Rambo, Shelly. *Resurrecting Wounds: Living in the Afterlife of Trauma*. Waco, TX: Baylor University Press, 2017.

Richard, Pablo. *Apocalypse: A People's Commentary on the Book of Revelation*. The Bible & Liberation Series. Maryknoll, NY: Orbis, 1995.

Sancken, Joni S. *Words That Heal: Preaching Hope to Wounded Souls*. The Artistry of Preaching. Nashville: Abingdon, 2019.

Sigmon, Amy. "Rev 21 Sermon." Belle Meade United Methodist Church, Nashville, Tennessee, December 29, 2019.

Sing the Journey: Hymnal—A Worship Book Supplement 1. Scottdale, PA: Faith and Life Resources, a Mennonite Publishing Network, 2005.

Smith, James K. A. *How (Not) to Be Secular: Reading Charles Taylor*. Grand Rapids: Eerdmans, 2014.

Spurgeon, Charles. *The Treasury of David*. The Spurgeon Archive. https://archive .spurgeon.org/treasury/ps137.php.

Taylor, Charles. *A Secular Age*. Cambridge: Belknap Press of Harvard University Press, 2007.

Thomas, Frank. "A Basin, Water Pitcher and a Towel." Riverside Church, New York City, Video, 15:00. https://www.youtube.com/watch?v=hkZXiB7S0VA.

———. *They Like to Never Quit Praisin' God: The Role of Celebration in Preaching*. Cleveland, OH: United Church, 1997.

———. "Why Not Trust God Again?" Mississippi Boulevard Christian Church, Memphis, Tennessee, October 12, 2013.

Thurman, Howard. *The Luminous Darkness: A Personal Interpretation of the Anatomy of Segregation and the Ground of Hope*. New York: Harper & Row, 1965.

Tierney, John, and Roy F. Baumeister. *The Power of Bad: How the Negativity Effect Rules Us and How We Can Rule It*. New York: Penguin, 2019.

Tutu, Desmond. *In God's Hands*. London: Bloomsbury, 2014.

VerMerris, Sarah. "Untitled Sermon." Preached August 2017 at North Hills Christian Reformed Church, Troy, Michigan.

Weiner, Eric. "Where Heaven and Earth Come Closer." *New York Times*, March 9, 2012.

Weingarten, Kaethe. *Common Shock: Witnessing Violence Every Day*. New York: Penguin, 2003.

Welker, Michael. *God the Spirit*. Minneapolis: Fortress, 1994.

Wilson, Paul Scott. *The Four Pages of the Sermon: A Guide to Biblical Preaching*. Nashville: Abingdon, 2018.

———. *God Sense: Reading the Bible for Preaching*. Nashville: Abingdon, 2001.

———. "How Has My Mind Changed." Lecture at What's New in Preaching Conference, Emmanuel College, Victoria University, Toronto, Ontario, March 12, 2019.

———. "Lecture on Preaching." Summer Preaching Seminar at United Theological Seminary, Dayton, Ohio, August 9–11, 2017.

———. *Setting Words on Fire: Putting God at the Center of the Sermon*. Nashville: Abingdon, 2008.

———. "Thin Resources and Thin Places: Doing Ministry in Troubled Times." *Ministry Matters*, March 24, 2020. https://www.ministrymatters.com/all /entry/10185/thin-resources-and-thin-places-doing-ministry-in-troubled -times.

Yoder, Mary Lehman, et al. "Promise: Essays by Readers." *Christian Century,* July 22, 2019. https://www.christiancentury.org/article/readers-write/promise -essays-readers.

Made in the USA
Columbia, SC
28 February 2024